Living Organism

Christopher Collins-Deynes

Disclaimer

The information contained in "Living Organism" is meant to serve as a comprehensive collection of strategies that the author of this eBook has researched. Summaries, strategies, tips, and tricks are the only recommendation by the author, and reading this eBook will not guarantee that one's results will exactly mirror the author's results. The author of the eBook has made all reasonable efforts to provide current and accurate information for the readers of the eBook. The author and its associates will not be held liable for any unintentional error or omissions that may be found. The material in the eBook may include information by third parties. Third-party materials comprise of opinions expressed by their owners. As such, the author of the eBook does not assume responsibility or liability for any third party material or opinions. Whether because of the progression of the internet, or the unforeseen changes in company policy and editorial submission guidelines, what is stated as fact at the time of this writing may become outdated or inapplicable later.

Contents

WHAT ARE LIVING ORGANNISM?

An organism refers to a living entity with an organized structure, capable of responding to stimuli, capable of reproducing, producing, adapting, and maintaining homeostasis. Therefore, an organism can be any animal, plant, fungus, protist, bacterium, or bow on earth. These organisms can be classified in different ways. One method is based on the number of cells in it. The two main groups are unicellular (eg bacteria, archaea, and protists) and multicellular (animals and plants). Organisms can also be classified according to their subcellular structures. Those with well-defined nuclei are called eukaryotes, while those not called prokaryotes. Both have genetic material but in different locations. In eukaryotes, the genetic material is found in the nucleus, while in prokaryotes it is known in a special place as the nucleoid. A modern classification system inhabits objects in three different areas: (1) Archaea (archaebacteria), (2) bacteria (eubacteria), and (3) eukaryotes (eukaryotes). Archaea and bacteria are prokaryotes, while Eucarya, as the name suggests, includes all eukaryotes. The scientific study of all organisms is called biology. Biology is a scientific field that aims to study the structure, function, distribution, and evolution of living things.

One of the most important sub-cellular components of a cell is the chromosome. Chromosomes contain genetic material. In bacteria and archaea, the chromosome is a circular DNA. In humans and other higher forms of organisms, it is like a wire, a linear DNA.

The part of DNA that is responsible for the physical and hereditary characteristics of an organism is called the gene. Genes encode amino acids, proteins, and RNA molecules. Protein is one of the major strains of biomolecules. Many of these are enzymes that mediate many biological processes.

Changes involving a gene can lead to mutations. As a result, new features may appear. Some mutations can be fatal or have side effects, but some mutations can also lead to beneficial results. Mutations can lead to evolution and natural selection. Acquiring new traits from these mutations can be beneficial to the survival of a species. For example, a lamb bacterium that is first sensitive to antibiotics may change and become resistant to antibiotics when it acquires new genes. In turn, an organism can change (through mutation) and adapt.

In addition to enzymes, many biological reactions require energy. The most common form of energy used by a living entity is adenosine triphosphate (ATP), the chemical energy used to stimulate various biological reactions. In plants and other photosynthetic organizations, light energy is converted into chemical energy by photosynthesis. Another way to generate energy is through cellular breathing. Cellular respiration is a cellular process in which carbohydrates are processed to produce chemical energy.

Living organisms are made up of cells. Cells are the structural and functional units of all living organisms, and a single cell can create multiple cells through a process called cell division.

Different organisms have different types of cells. Only the human body has different types of cells, such as blood cells, neurons, fat cells, etc. The shape and size of the cells depend on the actions they perform.

Some cells are joined together in shape and perform a specific function, such as neurons, which are mostly tree cells.

An organism is an animal that consists of a cell or group of cells and has the characteristics of life. They need to eat, grow and reproduce to guarantee the sustainability of their species. Organ systems work together to survive a living organism, even if a failure in one of these systems affects our lives.

HOW A LIVING ORGANISM IS DETERMINED ACCORDING TO THE LAWS OF SCIENCE OF TODAY

Although the science is constantly pushing the boundaries of our knowledge, we will never know everything. We don't even know what we don't know. For example, we can never understand how life was born. Although life can spread in the universe, this is not necessary for the continuity of turbulent matter. In other words, living organisms are not essential to the functioning of the universe. The laws of physics remain applicable regardless of the presence of life. As far as we know, life can only flow from existing life. This naturally raises the question of how the first living cells could be born. Life arose spontaneously from living nature once or several times? Can life between space travel be transferred between pliable planets? We just don't know. The mechanisms that led to the birth of a cell capable of autonomous growth and division are a mystery. This is a field of biology that requires a huge amount of research if there is ever evidence and no guarantee.

The rules of biology and science cannot be violated. These are not artificial human laws. These are natural laws that govern all life when living organisms evolve on our planet. Over the last few decades, people have changed our shared and shared biosphere through resource depletion and pollution. We know that these activities have upset the balance of nature and long-extinct species. The main types of pollution are because too many people are increasingly using too many non-renewable resources. Much of this damage is motivated by pleasure, greed, conflict, and a desire for power. We are all responsible for different levels.

Why do so many people attack the biosphere so primitively? Some ignore the result. They are not aware of the consequences of their actions. They do not realize that disturbances can have catastrophic consequences for our biosphere and all of us. They do not understand that natural selection is cruel and can cause great suffering and death. They think only for the moment and refuse to accept that it is their offspring that must be catastrophic. However, others are fully aware of the final consequences. And those of us who are aware of this need must act to pass on our knowledge to avoid or slow down our self-inflicted fate. However, research shows that we are entering our biosphere and the planet cannot accommodate our huge human population. We rely on natural resources to survive, but we do not live sustainably. This planet no longer needs consumption and pollution. It groans under the weight of our growing population. Entropy will make sense. It can be useful if everyone understands science and our natural world to understand what is needed for the survival of human species with an adequate quality of life. and the first step in this direction is to understand the basic laws of physics, chemistry, and biology and how they govern our biosphere, which is currently under attack and salvation. Without deep respect for nature and compassion for life, however, all life is probably insufficient. We need to be more caring, sensitive, and compassionate.

There are so many life forms around us, and even a simple single-celled organism is much more complex and purposeful than anything human ingenuity can bring. Matter and energy are basic life requirements, but they cannot be used to distinguish between living and nonliving systems. The central characteristic of all living beings is the "information" they contain and this information regulates all the vital processes and reproductive functions. The transfer of information plays a fundamental role in all living organisms. For example, when insects transmit pollen from one flower to another, it is mainly a process of transferring information genetic information istransmitted. The material actually used is not important. Although the information is important for life, information itself does not contain a complete description of life.

Enormous scientific advances have been made in recent

centuries and the time required to double our knowledge continues to decline. The sequencing of genomes of different species has been a necessary factor in the expansion of biological knowledge in recent decades. It has become central to the study of molecular and organic evolution. Technologies that allow genomics, molecular medicine, and computer science to make such rapid and interdependent advances are considered essential to understanding the earth's biosphere and its viability for future generations.

Biology has been at the forefront of science in recent years as we respond to our desire to understand the nature of living organisms and their evolutionary history. The following statements are based on a wealth of evidence. A fairly complete picture of life is possible only if each statement is embedded in the other. We ask for help from the international scientific community to inform us about changes and exceptions to the existing scientific dogma so that our concepts can be constantly developed. Only this approach allowed the drafting of certain basic biological laws. The first biological law: All living organisms follow the laws of thermodynamics. The second law of biology: All living organisms are made up of cells wrapped in a membrane. The third biological law: All living organisms are born in an evolutionary process.

The first biological law: All living organisms follow the laws of thermodynamics. This law is fundamental because the laws of the inanimate world determine the course of the universe. All organisms on all planets, including humans, must follow these laws. The laws of thermodynamics regulate energy conversions and mass distributions. Cells containing living organisms (see second law) are open systems through which both mass and energy can move through their membranes. Cells exist in open systems to obtain minerals, nutrients, and new genetic properties, while the final products of metabolism and toxic substances are extracted. Genetic variation, which results in part from gene transfer to prokaryotes and sexual reproduction in higher organisms, allows for dramatically increased phenotypic variability in a population and an accelerated rate of evolutionary deviation.

A consequence of the first law is that life requires the temporary creation of order, which of course is contrary to the second law of thermodynamics. By considering a fully enclosed system that includes materials and energy sources provided by the environment to sustain life, living organisms strictly affect the system according to this law and increase chance or chaos (entropy). The use of resources by living organisms thus increases the entropy of the world. A second consequence of the first law is that an organism died in biochemical equilibrium. When living organisms reach equilibrium with their environment, they no longer have a quality of life. Life depends on interconnected biochemical pathways for growth, macromolecular synthesis, and reproduction. Thus, not all life forms are balanced with their environment.

The second law of biology: All living organisms are made up of cells wrapped in a membrane. The surrounding membranes allow a natural separation between the living and non-living worlds. Viruses, plasmids, transposons, saws, and other selfish biological entities do not live. You can not play "only". For this purpose, they depend on a living cell. Therefore, they do not live by definition. One consequence of the second law is that the cell is the only structure that can grow and separate independently of other life forms. A second consequence of the second law is that all lives are programmed through genetic guidance. Genetic instructions are required for cell division, morphogenesis, and differentiation. From individual prokaryotes to normal or cancerous tissue in animals and multicellular plants, genetic instructions are needed to save lives.

The third biological law: All living organisms are born in an evolutionary process. This law correctly predicts the relationship between all living organisms on earth Explains everything

A SCIENTIFIC VIEW OF HOW LIVING ORGNISMS BEGINS

The question of whether living organisms over the centuries have received different answers from different religious and philosophical traditions can keep many people from deriving the question. But what does science tell us when life begins? One of the basic ideas of modern biology is that life is continuous, with living cells leading to new types of cells and ultimately new individuals. Therefore, we must first consider when a new human life begins, when the new cell, distinct from sperm and egg, appears.

The scientific basis for distinguishing one type of cell from another is based on two criteria: the differences in what is made of the molecular composition and the differences in the behavior of the cell. These two criteria are accepted and used by the entire scientific company. These are not "religious" beliefs or personal opinions. These are objective and verifiable scientific criteria that determine exactly when a new type of cell is formed.

Based on these criteria, the aggregation (or fusion) of sperm and egg cell produces a new type of cell, the zygote, or the single-celled embryo. Self-deception is a wellstudied and very fast event that occurs in less than a second. Because the zygote is the result of the fusion of two different cells, it contains all the components of the sperm and the egg, which is why this new cell has a unique molecular composition that is different from the two gametes. For example, the zygote that appears at the time of sperm fusion meets the first scientific criterion of being a new cell type: the molecular composition is different from the cells that generated it.

After the egg fuses with the sperm, things happen quickly in the zygote that doesn't normally occur in the sperm or egg. Within minutes, the zygote begins a change in the internal state that prevents additional sperm from binding to the cell surface for the next 30 minutes. The zygote, therefore, acts immediately to counteract the function of the gamete from which it is derived; While the "purpose" of sperm and egg is to find and fuse each other, the zygote's first action is to prevent other sperm from binding to the cell surface. It is clear that the zygote has entered a new behavioral pattern and thus fulfills the second scientific criterion for a new type of cell.

What is the nature of the new cell due to sperm-egg fusion?

More importantly, is the zygote just another human cell (like a liver or skin) or is it something else? Just as science distinguishes between different types of cells, it also clearly distinguishes between cells and organisms. Cells and organisms live, but organisms have unique properties that can reliably distinguish them from simple cells.

An organism is defined as a complex structure of interdependent and subordinate elements, the relationships and characteristics of which are largely determined by their function as a whole and an individual composed to carry out the activities of life through organs that function separately. is, but interdependent: a living being. This definition emphasizes the interaction of parts in the context of a coordinated whole as a distinguishing feature of an organism. Organisms are "living things". This is why another man is her name; an entity that is a complete human, rather than a part of a human.

Humans can be distinguished from human cells by using the same type of criteria that scientists use to distinguish different types of cells. A human (ie a human organism) consists of human parts (cells, proteins, RNA, DNA), but differs from a simple collection of cells because it has the characteristic molecular composition and behavior of 'an organism: it interacts dependent and coordinated way of 'carrying out the activities of life'.

WHAT MAKES LIVING ORGANISMS ALIVE?

All living organisms have different basic properties or functions: order, sensitivity or reaction to the environment, reproduction, adaptation, growth and development, homeostasis, energy processing, and evolution. All in all, these qualities serve to define life. Different sources may use slightly different terms to describe these characteristics, but the basic ideas are still there.

Organisms are highly organized and coordinated structures consisting of one or more cells. Even very simple single-celled organisms are surprisingly complex: atoms form molecules in each cell; they again form cellular organelles and other cellular inclusions in multicellular organisms.

The sensitivity of response to incentives

Organisms respond to various stimuli. For example, plants can lean against a light source, climb fences and walls, or respond to touch. Even small bacteria can travel to and from chemicals (a process called chemotaxis) or light (phototaxis).

REPRODUCTION

Unicellular organisms multiply by first duplicating their DNA and then dividing as the cell prepares to divide, forming two new cells. Multicellular organisms often produce specialized germ cells (reproductive cells) that form new individuals. During reproduction, DNA is transferred from an organism to the offspring of that organism. DNA contains instructions for creating all the physical features of an organism. This means that because parents and offspring share DNA, it ensures that the offspring are of the same species and will have similar characteristics like size and shape.

GROWTH AND DEVELOPMENT

All living things grow and / or change throughout their lives. For example, a person goes from child to adult and undergoes developmental processes such as puberty. Organisms grow and evolve by following specific instructions encoded by their genes (DNA). These genes provide instructions that control the growth and development of cells and ensure that the young growing species have many of the same characteristics as their parents.

Homeostasis and regulation

For the cells to function properly, they must have the right conditions, such as the right temperature, the right pH, and the right concentration of different chemicals. However, these conditions can be changed at any time. Organisms, thanks to constant homeostasis (literally "steady state") - the body's ability to maintain constant internal conditions - can maintain internal conditions within a limited range, despite changes in the environment, almost constantly.

For example, the body must regulate body temperature through a process called thermoregulation. Organisms that live in cold climates have body structures that help them withstand low temperatures and maintain body heat. Structures that support this type of insulation include fur, feathers, blush, and grease. In hot climates, organisms use techniques such as sweating in humans or shortness of breath in dogs to help them generate excess body heat.

Even the smallest organisms are complex and require many regulatory mechanisms to coordinate internal functions, respond to incentives, and control the environment. Two examples of internal body functions are the transport of nutrients and blood organs.

EVOLUTION

The theory of evolution, of biology, is that the various plant, animals, and other living species on Earth are derived from other existing types and that the distinguishable differences stem from changes in successive generations. The theory of evolution is one of the cornerstones of modern biological theory.

The variety of the living world is enormous. More than 2 million existing species of organisms have been identified and described; there are still plenty to discover - some estimates are from about a million to 30 million. Not only are the numbers, but also the incredible heterogeneity of size, shape, and lifestyle from modest bacteria to less than a thousandth of a millimeter in diameter to imposing red trees that are 100 feet (300 feet) taller. the earth rises and strikes thousands of tons; bacteria that live in hot springs near the boiling point of water, fungi, and algae that bloom at -23 ° C (-9 ° F) in the Antarctic ice mass and salt basins; and from giant worms discovered at the hydrothermal vents of the dark seabed to spiders and delphinium, located on the slopes of Mount Everest, more than 6,000 meters above sea level.

The geological time scale is 650 million years ago to the present day, showing important evolutionary events.

The geological time scale is 650 million years ago to the present day, showing important evolutionary events.

The almost endless variations of life are the fruits of the evolutionary process. All living beings are related to the descendants of their usual ancestors. Humans and other mammals are derived from strange creatures that lived more than 150 million years ago; mammals, birds, reptiles, amphibians, and fish are shared as ancestors by water worms that lived 600 million years ago; and all plants and animals are derived from bacteria-like microorganisms that originated more than 3 billion years ago. Biological evolution is a succession process with modification. The genders of organizations vary from generation to generation; diversity is created because the descendants of ordinary ancestors differ over time.

They also claim that organisms come through evolution, and this was a particular scientific explanation, essentially correct but incomplete as to how evolution takes place and why organisms have properties such as wings, eyes, and kidneys. which are structured to perform specific functions. The basic concept of his exhibition was natural selection. Natural selection occurs because individuals with beneficial traits, such as acute vision or faster bones, live better, and produce more offspring than individuals with less favorable traits. Genetics, a science born in the 20th century, explores in detail how natural selection works and has led to the development of a modern theory of evolution. A related scientific discipline, molecular biology, has provided an advanced knowledge of biological evolution since the 1960s and has made it possible to examine detailed problems that until recently seemed completely unattainable - such as what genes humans and chimpanzees might have in common. (about 1-2% of the units that make up the genes differ from each other).

To my knowledge, evolution, as it usually refers to living things, To discuss human evolution.

GENETICS

Genetics is the study of how hereditary traits are passed on from parents to offspring. People have long noticed that family traits tend to be similar. The most important effects of genetic inheritance were not scientifically investigated until the middle of the 19th century.

NATURAL SELECTION

In almost all population groups, individuals tend to produce more offspring than are needed to replace their parents. If every born person were to live and reproduce even more offspring, the population would collapse. Overcrowding leads to competition for resources.

DEFINITON OF ECOLOGY

Ecology is a branch of biology that investigates how organisms interact with their environment and other organisms. Each organism has a complex relationship with other organisms in the genus and with different types of organisms. These complex interactions lead to different selection pressures on organisms. The combined pressure leads to natural selection, which leads to the development of species populations. Ecology is the study of these forces, their causes, and the complex relationship between organisms and between organisms and organisms and their non-living environment.

Scientists can look at ecology with different lenses, from the microscopic molecular level to the entire planet. These different types of ecology will be discussed later. At all ecological levels, the focus is on selective pressure, which is causing evolutionary change. This pressure comes from several sources, and there are several methods to locate and quantify this data.

In the field of ecology, there are many undergraduate students. While the following types of ecology are shared at the level of the organism, the ecologist specializes in certain aspects of each area. Cognitive ecology, for example, is a branch of organism ecology that studies the mental processes of animals. Other ecologists study only the interactions between humans and the rest of bio that are known in humanecologor environmental science. Still other environmentalists focus on the interaction between organisms and abiotic factors that influence development, such as nutrients and toxins. Ecology is a big field. Below is just a selection of the different things that scientists in ecology study.

TYPES OF ECOLOGY

Type 1: Molecular Ecology

At the molecular level, the study of ecology focuses on the production of proteins, how these proteins affect the body and the environment, and how the environment affects the production of different proteins. In known organisms, DNA causes different proteins that interact with each other and with the environment to replicate in DNA. These interactions lead to several very complex organizations. The molecular ecologist investigates how these proteins are produced, how they affect the body and the environment and how they are affected by the environment.

Type 2: Ecology Of Organisms

The study of organizational ecology goes a step further and addresses individual organizations and their interaction with other organizations and the environment. Although organizational biology is a department of ecology, it is still a vast field. There are different interactions in the life of each organism, and it is impossible to study them. Many scientists who study the ecology of organisms focus on one aspect of the body, e.g. B. how it behaves or how it processes nutrients from the environment.

The study of ethology or behavior can also be examined as ecology. Instead of analyzing certain behaviors in animals, behavioral ecologists look at how these behaviors affect the development of the organism and how the environment puts the behaviors under pressure. For example, a behavioral ecologist can look at how an eagle hunts its prey and determine which behaviors lead to success and which fail. In this way, the scientist can represent the forces that make Adler act like them. This information can be of great importance in the development of conservation plans for wildlife protection.

Type 3: Population Ecology

The next organizational level is for organisms, population groups, groups of similar organisms. Due to the great variety of life on earth, different species have developed very different strategies to work with peers or similar organisms. Some species compete directly with other species, while other organisms have close ties and work together on resources. A branch of ecology, social ecology, examines organisms such as bees and dogs and trades on the colony or herd. The complex interactions between these organisms and their environment are translated into selective forces that differ from the animal forces that compete with other species. Scientists speculate that humans are just as communicative as growing successes in human society. The population ecologist examines organic populations and their complex interactions with the environment and other population groups.

Type 4: Community Ecology

Different communities living in the same area create organic communities. These communities create different niches or spaces that organisms can occupy. For example, there are different niches in the wheat field. Wheat is found in the sun's rays and soil nutrients. Various nutrients nourish the nutrients that wheat collects. Some bacteria occupy a niche in the roots, where they convert nitrogen into a plant. The community ecologist examines these complex interactions and the selective pressures they create. Sometimes community bodies start a coefficient in which one or more species develop in response to each other. It is seen in many species, from bees and flowers they pollinate to predators and prey they eat.

MUTATION

Transformation, alteration of the genetic material of a living organism, or a virus that is more or less permanent and can be transmitted to the offspring of the cell or virus. The genome of organisms consists of DNA and a viral genome can be DNA or RNA; see Heritage: the physical origin of inheritance.) DNA can be a mutation of the DNA cells of a multicellular organism (somatic mutation) which causes DNA. thereplication is transferred to the coating cells, leading to a sector or patch of cells with an abnormal function, such as cancer. Each cell carrying the mutation can lead to a single progeny in eggs or sperm (mutations of the germline), which often leads to severe dysfunctions, for example in the case of human genetic diseases such as cystic fibrosis. The mutations result from accidents during normal DNA chemical transactions, often during replication, or due to exposure to high-energy electromagnetic radiation (such as ultraviolet light or X-rays) or radiation from highly reactive particles or chemicals in the environment. Since mutations are random changes, most are expected to be harmful, but some may be helpful in certain environments. In general, the mutation is the most important source of genetic diversity, the raw material for evolution through natural selection.

A UNIVERSAL LAW OF ALL LIVING ORGANISM

Despite the infinite variety of lives, many of the most important characteristics of living species, such as growth and metabolism, are subject to universal laws, but not as previously thought.

The diversity of life is frightening. While biologists tend to focus on the diversity of species and their survival, what suits them may be more interesting than what separates them. In the age of big data and the flow of information, it is now possible to fully comprehend this diversity, an informative universal trait that is common to all beings, large and small.

Learn more about sizes

It was already known that there are simple mathematical laws that bind the body mass of an organism to some of its most basic properties, such as metabolism, growth, mortality, and abundance. Within the large taxonomic groups of living things, these characteristics are linked to body mass by a law of power whose exponent often approaches. Thus the metabolic increase of an organism increases according to its body mass brought to force by ¾, which means that the metabolism does not grow faster than the mass. These are scaling laws that have interested in evolutionary biologists and environmentalists for decades. However, the relationships between the four basic properties of organisms (metabolism, growth rate, mortality, and abundance) and all living things have never been systematically studied.

For example, the product of an organism's metabolism and abundance is independent of body size, which means that the cumulative metabolism of all organisms of the same species is more or less stable, regardless of size.

Growth is at most

With the confirmation and generalization of universal laws that have been demonstrated or predicted in the past, the results of our study are also an important challenge for one of the most important theories in ecology, known as the "metabolic theory of ecology". Hypothesis provides experts with one of the basic frameworks for understanding the relationship between the most important demographic and functional characteristics of a species and its body mass, based on the idea that the metabolism of an organism is determined by the acquisition and use of available resources, and thus constitute the main limitation of many other important traits, including the rate at which organic growth and development.

However, one of the main conclusions of our study is that the opposite is true: the growth rate of an organism appears to regulate its metabolism. The growth rate is actually related to body mass by a scaling law with a bishop of ¾, and this ratio is extremely stable in all taxonomic groups. In contrast, metabolic rates follow this law only in all large groups, and not for individuals belonging to different taxonomic groups. Ultimately, growth and not metabolism appear to be the major biological constraint that regulates the large life dimensions.

As growth underlies all biological and ecological processes, from the development of cancerous tumors to the production of our biological resources, the global carbon cycle, and population dynamics, it is possible to determine the factors affecting the growth of the living system. necessary.

Wherever you look, whatever kind of living system you see, they seem to be following the same growth law. Although we do not yet know the biological boundaries of this universal law, we do know that it has far-reaching consequences. It offers a new perspective on the most fundamental features of life and the extraordinary unity that moves through a variety of living organisms.

Fossils

Fossils are the remains or traces of the remains of ancient organisms. Fossils are not the remains of the organism! These are rocks.

A fossil can protect an entire organism or only a part of it. Bones, shells, feathers, and leaves can become fossils.

Fossils can be very large or very small. Microfossils are only visible under a microscope. Bacteria and pollen are microfossils. Macrofossils can be several meters long and weigh several tons. Macrofossils can be petrified trees or dinosaur bones.

Life

The concept of organisms focuses on the 'life' trait. Life is a difficult term to define the quality that distinguishes living organisms from dead organisms and non-living things. Although there is no consensus on definition, the biological properties of organisms known in the world (plants, animals, fungi, protists, archaea and bacteria) are based on carbon and water and are cellular with a complex organization that consumes energy. and metabolism, the ability to grow, maintain homeostasis, respond to stimuli, reproduce and make various environmental adaptations.

Not all life definitions consider all of these essential qualities. For example, the ability to catch up with change is often seen as an essential quality of life. This definition especially includes viruses that do not fit the narrower definitions because they are vinegar and do not metabolize. Additional life definitions may include theoretical carbon-free life.

Apart from the biological representations of matter, several philosophical perspectives, especially the Arastotelian soul theory and modern vitality, add that living organisms have an internal dimension or character that gives them quality of life. I do not agree with the modern biological mechanism, the phenomena explain life only concerning the external principles of chemistry and physics.

CHARACTERISTICS OF AN ORGANISM

Organisms (before death) have many universal properties,

including that they consist of cells; transmitting their inheritance with an almost universal genetic code; the environment needs energy to exist, grow and reproduce; and maintain their internal environment; Further. These are the common traits identified by biologists that distinguish between living and non-living organisms. Inanimate people may have some of these characteristics, but not all of them.

The cells.

Except for viruses, all organisms contain cells. A cell is the basic unit of life and the smallest unit that can perform all life processes, including maintenance, growth, and even self-repair.

Carbon-based biochemistry. Living organisms are characterized by general carbon-based biochemistry. All organisms inherit their heritage through genetic material, which is based on nucleic acids such as **DNA**, using an almost universal genetic code. Every cell, whether simple or complex, uses nucleic acids to transfer, store and store the information needed to produce proteins.

Organization. Living organisms are organized at the molecular and cellular level. Energy and materials are organized from the environment, such as the internal structure of a cell or the organization of multicellular organisms in tissues, organs and systems. In essence, living organisms reverse the entropy.

Energy and metabolism. All living things need energy from the environment to exist, grow and reproduce.

Development and growth. Living beings grow and develop as they age. This involves maintaining a higher synthesis rate compared to catalysis, with the growth of the organism occurring through cell proliferation and division. A growing organism grows in all its parts rather than picking up one material.

Homeostasis: All living organisms, both cellular and multicellular, display homeostasis. Homeostasis possesses an open system to regulate its internal environment to maintain a stable condition.

Response to stimuli. All living organisms react with the environment.

Adjustment. Living organisms have characteristics that provide a survival / reproductive advantage in an environment. that is, they have adaptations to the environment. Living organisms show variability in these adaptations so that species can survive in a changing or changing environment.

Reproduction is the ability to produce new organisms. It is important to note that reproduction is primarily a species-level trait. Although many people do not reproduce a specific species, probably because they are associated with specialized sterile complexes (such as ants) or are sterile for other reasons, including age or disease, they are still considered life forms.

BASIC GROUPS

Two main groups of organisms can be distinguished.

Unicellular And Multicellular. Some simple life forms, such as Paramecium, consist of a single cell during their life cycle and are called unicellular organisms. Multicellular organisms such as a whale or a tree can contain billions of differentiated cells and cells that perform specific functions. The term complex organism describes any organism that consists of more than one cell.

Another major difference is between **prokaryotes** and **eukaryotes**. The prokaryotic-eukaryotic rupture is widely recognized as an important missing link in evolutionary history. It is generally accepted that prokaryotes represent two separate domains, called bacteria and archaea, which are not closer to each other than eukaryotes.

VIRUS

SARS-CoV-2 "Coronavirus"

Viruses are generally not considered organisms because they cannot reproduce or metabolize 'independently'. However, this controversy is problematic because even some parasites and endosymbiotic cannot live independently. Although viruses contain enzymes and molecules that are characteristic of living organisms, they cannot reproduce outside a host cell, and most of their metabolic processes require a host and its genetic machinery.

Superorganism

A superorganism is an organism that consists of many organisms. It is usually a social unit of eusocial animals in which the division of labor is highly specialized and in which individuals cannot survive independently for long. Ants are the best-known example of such a superorganism.

Thermoregulation

A trait normally exhibited by individual organisms, does not occur in individuals or small groups of honeybees of the Apismellifera species. When these bees congregate in groups of 5,000 to 40,000, the colony can thermoregulate as a group.

Macromolecules

The compounds that makeup organisms can be broken down into macromolecules and other smaller molecules. The four groups of macromolecules are nucleic acids, proteins, carbohydrates, and lipids. Nucleic acids (especially deoxyribonucleic acid or DNA) store genetic data as a series of nucleotides. The different sequences of the organism are determined by the specific sequence of the four different types of nucleotides (adenine, cytosine, guanine, and thymine). The sequence is divided into codons, each containing a specific sequence of three nucleotides and corresponding to a specific amino acid. Therefore, it encodes a DNA sequence for a specific protein that returns in a specific way due to the chemical properties of the amino acids of which it is composed, thus fulfilling a specific function.

The following protein functions have been identified:

Enzymes that dilute all reactions in the metabolism;

structural proteins, such as tubulin or collagen;

Regulatory proteins, such as transcription factors or cycles, that regulate the cell cycle;

Signal molecules or their receptors, such as some

hormones and their receptors

Protective proteins, which can range from antibodies in the immune system to toxins (eg snake smoke toxins) to proteins that contain unusual amino acids, such as canavanine.

Lipids are the cell membrane, a barrier that holds everything in the cell and prevents compounds from entering and leaving the cell freely. In some multicellular organisms, they work to store energy and mediate communication between cells. Carbohydrates store and transport energy in some organisms, but are easier to break down than lipids.

Structure

Each organism consists of monomeric units called cells; some contain single (single-celled) cells and some contain multiple (multicellular) units. Multicellular organisms can specialize cells to perform specific functions, one of these groups of cells in the tissue which consists of the four basic types of epithelium, nerve tissue, muscle tissue, and connective tissue. Some types of tissue work together in the form of an organ to perform a specific function (such as pumping blood to the heart or as an environmental barrier such as the skin). This model goes to a higher level, with more organs acting as an organ system to facilitate reproduction and digestion. Many multicellular organisms consist of different organ systems that are in line to make life possible.

A non-cellular life

Are viruses living things? This question has brought a long debate among biologists. Some consider living things to be viruses because they appear to be alive in the host. They have genetic material, it repeats and develops through natural selection. Others, however, do not accept them as living beings because they are essentially dead outside their host. Viruses cannot reproduce independently. They rely on host machines to do this. Therefore, viruses are not fully alive or non-living. When outside their host, viruses become inactive and appear lifeless. Once in their hosts, they became active, able to use and replicate host structures. Viroids are another group that looks non-cellular. These are contagious and pathogenic short strands of a single-stranded circular RNA

THE ENVIROMENT SHAPE OF OGANISM

Organisms live in almost every environment on earth, from warm vents at the bottom of the oceans to icy regions of the Arctic. Each environment provides resources and constraints that determine the appearance of the species that live in it, as well as the strategies that this species uses to survive and reproduce. Some of the widest patterns of environmental disparity arise from the way our planet revolves around the sun and the worldwide distribution of sunlight. In the tropics, where there is sunlight all year round, the temperature is warm and plants can constantly photosynthesize as long as water and nutrients are available. In polar regions, where solar radiation is limited by the season, the average temperature is much lower and organisms have to deal with longer periods when photosynthesis stops.

In ecosystems, natural resources and constraints determine the structure and physiology of an organism. The variety of chemical elements present is one of the oldest environmental legacies in the world. At birth, the earth found a carbon atom that produced stars that burned long before our sun formed. These carbon atoms, with their unique ability to build four-way chains and bonds with other elements, are the backbone of all organic molecules living today. Nitrogen and phosphorus are important elements in living organisms, where they play a key role in the composition of proteins, nucleic acids and energetic compounds. These elements are not always readily available to organisms, so nutritional restrictions can severely limit biological strategies. Inert nitrogen gas, for example, forms 78% of the Earth's atmosphere, but the forms of nitrogen that can be easily used by organisms are generally much rarer in terrestrial ecosystems. ecosystems. However, with fierce competition for nitrogen and other elements, environmentalists find that dietary restrictions limit life in many environments.

Organisms are further shaped by the physical characteristics of the environment in which they live, including the density and temperature of the environment. Marine mammals such as stellate sea lions (Eumetopiasjubatus), for example, have developed streamlined bodies that move efficiently in water, which is more than 700 times closer than air, but slows down on land. As a result, lions sleep on the shore, but mostly search for food in the water, where their speed is optimal.

Ecologists also study how temperature affects the ecology and evolution of a species. Organisms usually slow down or freeze when cold, but they overheat and lose function as the temperature rises. So many species have developed traits that help them protect themselves from extreme temperatures and affect their ecology. While sea lions, for example, rely on thick layers of fat for insulation, seaweeds (Enhydralutris) that swim in the same cold water need an extraordinarily thick layer to retain heat. As a result, seaweeds spend more time tending to themselves, and their thick fur attracted hunters who threatened to disappear. On Earth, research shows that cold-blooded plants and animals develop a dark color and position themselves to maximize the increase in solar energy in cold weather. In warmer regions, studies show that animals can avoid the sun's rays, protect plants by wiping large amounts of water, maximize airflow through the leaves, or remain inactive until the temperature returns late. Some temperature changes can be surprising. For example, scientists recently found that grasses growing near geothermal openings absorb heat from a virus in a fungus in their roots.

The availability of water further determines the ecological dynamics of the world. Water ecosystems developed early in life and all living cells still need water to function. Temperature affects the availability of water, due to very cold climates, water is frozen and unavailable, and evaporates rapidly in very hot climates. Ecological studies on relationships with water show that organisms use an astonishing variety of strategies to capture and maintain water supply. For example

Because of this limitation and because energy is lost at all stages of food transmission, low productivity ecosystems tend to support consumers with less biomass than higher productivity systems. Ecologists have identified this condition as a possible reason that the greater biodiversity in tropical rainforests is more productive than in less productive systems such as deserts. Within societies, environmental variability can lead to complex variations in ecological dynamics. For example, researchers have recently found that rising temperature rises can significantly increase the aggression of some reef fish. These behavioral changes can increase exposure to fish to predators and other risks.

Because the environment is dynamic and diverse, ecologists recognize that there is not a single ecological trait or strategy that makes an organism "better". All living populations and species are constantly changing as a result of pressure from other organisms and changes in the earth's geology and climate. Over time, this dance of evolutionary interactions has created an incredible array of organisms that are interdependent in the world and competition with each other. To recreate the earth's ecological history, ecologists and other scientists are looking for data of all kinds, including tree rings describing ancient drought patterns, ice cores containing bubbles from the earth's former atmosphere, and DNA contained in the thousands of ancient bones. These data show how organisms have responded to environmental changes, including the hardship caused by the meteoromers that helped mammals age 65 million years ago.

ORGANISM SHAPE THE ENVIROMENT

The environment is dynamic, as physical processes stimulate

changes in the properties of the earth over time. However, research shows that life itself changes that are just as important to the environment. Because other organisms are part of everyone's environment, the distribution of species can dramatically change the ecological interactions within communities. In some cases, the loss of native species or the introduction of alien species can threaten the survival of other organisms. As a result, the conservation of endangered organisms and the control of invasive species are a major concern.

Ecologists have found that interactions between organisms take different forms. In antagonistic relationships, organisms compete for resources, spread diseases to their neighbors, or eat each other. In more mutual associations, one organism houses another organ; two organisms exchange resources or dependencies become closer as the relationship between specialized pollinators and flowers develops together. In some cases, other species are also cultivated. Ecologists, for example, recently discovered that the reef seawater plant tends to create underwater gardens where predators remove and hunt less desirable alpine species. In other cases, species with large structures become habitats for smaller organisms. The human digestive tract, for example, contains so many bacteria that there are ten times as many cells in the human body. A promised area of microbial ecology and medicine is now the study of how microbes in the digestive tract affect their host. On a larger scale, the evolutionary emergence of flowering plants (angiosperms) and the development of large rainforests created new environments in which animals experimented with new ecological strategies. Scientists suggest that the development of the open branch structure of rainforest trees contributed to the development of the forepaw structure in monkeys, making it possible to swing from tree to tree and leave people with skill behind.

Research shows that organisms have an additional ability to change the environment by changing water supply and flow, energy, and elements on a small and large scale. The atmosphere changes and creates the earth's ozone layer. The ozone layer, therefore, reduces the UV radiation on the earth's surfaces and helps to protect the organisms on earth from potentially deadly UV radiation. Today, plant life controls a large part of the flow of energy and water between the earth and the atmosphere. Scientists estimate that the removal of all plants from the earth will be reduced by 50% by removing all plants from the ground. Animals also play an important role in influencing the physical characteristics of ecosystems. Recent work shows, for example, that subterranean termites in Kenya increase grassland productivity and biodiversity over large areas by increasing soil fertility in supplementary crops. In the 21st century, the most important environmental problems are related to human manipulation of the world environment. Future research will address the conflict between human needs for food, fuel, and fiber and the conservation of natural biodiversity and ecological function.

FIVE KINGDOM OF LIVING THINGS

Statements

In the past, there were two categories of all living things, namely plants and animals. Standing organisms are classified as plants. On the contrary, animals included all living things that could move. In time, scientists discovered other living organisms that could not be found in plants or animals. Thus was born the Linnaean system of taxonomic classification. Let us briefly talk about each of the five kingdoms of living things and the organisms that are classified under them.

Monera Kingdom

Organisms: bacteria, cyanobacteria or blue-green algae (BGA) and spirochete

Number of species identified: 4000 - 10000

Nutritional methods: absorption of food by the cell wall, chemotherapy and photosynthesisLiving things in the kingdom of Monera are unicellular prokaryotes (organisms that do not contain membrane-bound nuclei). However, cyanobacteria are a type of organism that sits between algae (it contains chlorophyll) and bacteria (it is prokaryotic). Some members of the same organism may possibly form chains and colonies. In addition, some species in this group are characterized by the least sensitive areas, such as B. deep oceans, hot springs, and acid pools.

Kingdom Protestants

Organisms: protozoa, slimy form and some unicellular algae

Number of species identified: 80,000

Nutritional methods: absorption, intake, and photosynthesis.

Protist or Protoctista consists of monolingual eukaryotic organisms in which cellular organs bind to cells. It contains organisms other than plants and animals. Simply put, living things classified as Protestant are unusual and diverse forms that cannot be divided into any of the remaining four kingdoms. This kingdom contains, for example, amoeba (protozoa), the simplest organism in the world, and giant algae (algae). It occurs in aquatic and rural habitats.

Kingdom Champions

Organisms: molds, yeasts, molds, soot, poisonous fungi, and fungi.

Number of species identified: 70,000 - 72,000

Diet method: uptake of nutrients from dead and decayed organic matter

A fungus is a group of multicellular, eukaryotic, immobilized, and ubiquitous organisms that form hyphens and mycelium. Many species look like plants, so they used to be grouped together by accident. Unlike plants, members of the fungal kingdom do not have chlorophyll. The size can vary from small microscopic yeasts to very large mushrooms. Fungi play an important role in keeping the environment clean by feeding dead organisms and distributing nutrients in the ecosystem.

Kingdom Plantae

Organisms: algae, ferns, flowering plants, and non-flowering plants

Number of species identified: 270,000

Diet method: photosynthesis

Kingdom Plantae contains multi-, eukaryotic, and immobile things. These organisms contain the photosynthetic pigment chlorophyll. As a result, all plants except unicellular algae are assigned to this kingdom. They synthesize their own food through photosynthesis, i.e. Synthesis of foods from carbon dioxide and water in the presence of sunlight. Plants can grow on land and in water (freshwater and brine).

Animalia Kingdom

Organisms: sponges, insects, worms, fish, reptiles, amphibians, birds and mammals

Number of species identified: 1,326,239 - 1,500,000

Feeding method: feeding on other organisms

Animalia is a group of multicellular, eukaryotic, and mobile living things. Members of Animalia are similar to members of Plantae in their cellular composition. In addition to the locomotive section, an important distinguishing point is that animals do not have chlorophyll and cannot synthesize food alone. Therefore, they feed by ingestion. They can feed on plants and other living things.

The life sciences focus on the models, processes, and relationships of living organisms. Life is self-sustaining, self-sustaining, self-reproducing, and evolving. It works according to the laws of the physical world as well as genetic programs. Life scientists use observation, experiments, hypotheses, tests, models, theory, and technology to study how life works. The study of life extends beyond the boundaries of individual molecules, organisms, and ecosystems to the entire biosphere, that is, to all life on earth. It examines processes that take place over time scales ranging from eyes to those over billions of years. Living systems are interconnected and interactive. Although living organisms respond to the physical environment or the atmosphere, they have radically changed the earth over time. Rapid advances in the life sciences help to find biological solutions to societal problems related to nutrition, energy, health, and the environment.

From viruses and bacteria to plants, fungi, and animals, the variety of millions of life forms on earth is incredible. Without an agreement on principles, it would be difficult to understand the living world and apply the concept to problem-solving. A key principle in the life sciences is that all organisms participate in the evolution and that evolutionary processes result in great diversity in the biosphere. There are differences in species as well as between species. However, what we learn about the function or processes of genes or cells in an organism applies to other organisms because of their ecological interactions and evolutionary relationships. Evolution and its underlying genetics

The mechanisms of heredity and variability are fundamental

to understanding the unity and diversity of life on earth.

The committee developed four fundamental ideas that reflect general principles in the life sciences. These basic ideas are essential for a conceptual understanding of the life sciences and enable students to understand emerging research. We start at the organism level and treat a wide range of processes and structures on scales ranging from components as small as individual atoms to the organ systems needed to sustain life. Then we expand our attention to think about organisms in their environment - how they deal with living (biotic) and physical (abiotic) aspects of the environment. This chapter then examines how organisms reproduce, transmit genetic information to their offspring, and how these mechanisms alter the variability and thus the diversity of species. Finally, the basic ideas of life sciences conclude that evolution can explain how the observed diversity within species left the diversity of life between species through a process of descent with adaptable modification. Evolution also emphasizes the remarkable similarity in the basic characteristics of each species.

Molecules for organisms: Structures and processes deal with the configuration of individual organisms and how these structures function to support life, growth, transport, and reproduction. The first central idea is based on the uniform principle that cells are the basic unit of life.

Ecosystems: interactions, energy, and dynamics study the interactions between organisms and their physical environment. These include how organisms acquire resources, how their environment changes, how environmental factors influence organisms and ecosystems, how social interactions and group behaviors take place within and between them, species, and how all these factors together determine the functioning of the ecosystem.

All living organisms follow chemical and physical laws. The chemistry of life is largely organic, occurs mainly in aqueous solution over a narrow temperature range, and is very complex. Polymer molecules (nucleic acids, lipids, and proteins) coordinate all chemical reactions in living organisms, the unique chemical and physical properties of which ensure their organization, growth, and reproduction. Although nucleic acids are the central repository of genetic information in all cells, the architecture and function of individual cells, tissues, and organisms are dependent on proteins. For many of these proteins, their specific point of action is far removed from their biosynthesis. It is therefore important that the cell has precise mechanisms for the correct concentration of proteins. This protein target problem has been identified as a central problem in modern biology for the past 20 years, and in fact, specific target mechanisms have been identified for different subcellular compartments. It works on special macromolecular protein machines dedicated to the identification and transport of proteins. The extent of these targeted events is indicated, as almost half of the proteins of the cell are transposed or translocated into a membrane. Basic chemical energy, a small molecule called ATP, provides energy for these and other processes in cells (motion, active transport of molecules, and biosynthesis of large macromolecules from simpler molecules). This universal energy carrier (called fuel for the cell) is produced in special compartments in the cell called mitochondria. Without mitochondria, a large number of organisms, including humans, animals, fungi, and plants, would not be able to use oxygen to draw energy from their supporting subunits. Mitochondria are made up of about a thousand different proteins. Interestingly, almost all outside the mitochondria are synthesized and then introduced into the mitochondria. The import process is therefore very important for the proper functioning of the cell and many diseases in humans are related to dysfunction of the mitochondrial input system. We investigate the orchestra and the coordination of the protein input process in mitochondria on special macromolecular arrangements and how the chemical and physical properties of these polymer complexes guarantee a good biological function.

Metabolism -: the sum of chemical reactions that take place in every cell of a living organism that provides energy for important processes and the synthesis of new organic matter.

Living organisms are unique in the sense that they can extract energy from their environment and use it to perform activities such as movement, growth, development, and reproduction. But how do living organisms, or their cells, extract energy from their environment, and how do cells use this energy to synthesize and compose the components of which they are made?

The answers to these questions lie in the chemical reactions mediated by enzymes that take place in living substances (metabolism). Hundreds of coordinated, multi-stage reactions, driven by energy and/or solar energy, eventually transform readily available materials into molecules needed for growth and maintenance.

The physical and chemical properties of the ingredients of living things discussed in this article can be found in the carbohydrate articles; cell; hormone; lipids; photosynthesis; and proteins.

A summary of metabolism

The unity of life

At the level of cellular organization, the major chemical processes of all living substances are similar, if not identical. This applies to animals, plants, fungi, or bacteria; where variations occur (such as in the secretion of antibodies by certain forms), the various processes are only variations on general themes. Thus, all living matter consists of large molecules called proteins, which provide coordinated support and movement, as well as the storage and transport of small molecules and as catalysts enable chemical reactions that take place rapidly and specifically moderate temperatures, relatively low concentrations, and conditions. neutral (ie not acidic or basic). Proteins are made up of about 20 amino acids, and just as the 26 letters of the alphabet can be put together in specific ways to form words of different lengths and meanings, there are tens or even hundreds of the 20 "letters". amino acids can be linked. to form specific proteins. Also, the parts of protein molecules involved in performing similar functions in different organisms often contain the same amino acid sequences.

HOW THE CONCEPTS OF SCIENCE HAVE BEEN INCORRECT AND DEBUNKED

Two people are discussing a scientific topic, and the person who is against the general scientific view is supported by an adversary who is conducting several peer-reviewed studies. How does he get out? Simply put, he just utters the words, "Well, scientists were wrong in the past, so they might be wrong now." After saying these undeniable words, the debate ends and the anti-scientist goes and ponders. He was just using a logically invalid escape, which only shows how weak and untenable his position is.

The first problem with this argument is simply that it is a forgery bug (or ad hominem, depending on how precisely it is used). Just because scientists have made mistakes in the past doesn't mean you can blindly reject all evidence and arbitrarily assume that it is now wrong. The rules of logic tell us that this argument is not a good one.

The second problem is one of the most important. Of course, scientists have been wrong in the past because science itself is a process in which other scientists prove otherwise. This is how science works. It would be terrible if scientists never made a mistake because that would mean that science stopped and went no further. But the most important thing is: scientists are always proven wrong by other scientists! Great scientific principles are not overthrown by people with no scientific training sitting on their couch and wondering! New scientific discoveries have been made by scientists, not bloggers, not people who have never entered a laboratory. There is no universe in which a person's illiterate opinion is as valid as the results of countless peer-reviewed studies.

Next, we come to a core problem with the basic claim of this argument. Most of the time I hear this argument accompanied by the claim that "scientists thought the earth was flat," but did scientists believe that? You see, the term "science" is relatively new. Almost all of the examples I hear of the supposedly flawed beliefs of scientists come from an era of science as we know it. Science today is a very careful, systematic process that allows us to be very confident in our results. For example, there have only been statistical analyzes with which we can test our hypotheses quantitatively for 100 years. There is simply no comparison between "scientists" who thought the earth was flat and scientists today. "Scientists" were no different from alchemists at that time. They did not use the rigorous scientific methods that we now use.

So if we are to say that "scientists made mistakes in the past and shouldn't trust them today," we have to refer to roughly the past 100 years. Now let's ask: "Have scientists been wrong about anything in the past 100 years?" Of course, they said too many things. Great strides have been made in almost every area of science over the past 100 years as discoveries have replaced outdated hypotheses. Note, however, that this argument is used against scientific theories and concepts that contain an overwhelming amount of evidence. It is not used against any particular cladogram showing the evolutionary relationships between turtles, but against the entire theory of evolution. It is not used against any particular model of climate change, but against the idea that humans can change the climate. So the question is, "In the last 100 years, have scientists made the wrong choice about something very important that they were extremely certain of (something like evolutionary theory or the usefulness of vaccines)?" The answer is ... wrong. The changes that Einstein's theory of relativity made to Newtonian physics relate to the direct example, but even then Newton was not wrong, it was incomplete, and relativity was introduced at the beginning of the 100 year period we are talking about. So unless you think about it anymore, the gist of this argument is not even correct.

1. The earth is flat - scientific theories are wrong

Contrary to popular knowledge, some people, including scientists, believe that the earth is flat rather than spherical as we know it. Members of the Flat Universe Society claim that the earth appears to be 'flat'. They believe that there is a secret government agency that has made everyone believe that the earth is accurate. So they can hide some conspiracy.

According to this misinterpretation of scientific misconceptions, day and night cycles are NASA and the moon and sun are their orbits around the flat planet, 32 miles above the flat disk we call home - like trying to stay calm and not be aware of the real world in which we live.

2. The earth is empty - replaces the theories of science

This scientific theory, Hollow Earth Theory, is a concept in which the planet Earth is partially or completely hollow and contains large internal space. Although many have rejected this concept. But some scientists are still working hard to prove this myth. This theory goes back to the days of the Greeks and there is evidence that the dead spent their afterlife in the center of the planet.

According to the legend of Tibetan Buddhists, an ancient city in the heart of the world is called Shamballa. Although modern science has since advanced this theory, it is wonderful to imagine the possibilities if this amazing place would be real.

3. worm cause rot and decay.

Medieval magicians all over the world have constantly come up with crazy solutions and theories, some of which have evolved modern medicine as we know it, and some of which are just crazy ideas that do not make sense to us. Hundreds of years ago, oral hygiene was not important: with an average life expectancy of fewer than 30 people, most people survived their teeth.

Unlike today, we live more than 100 and need our teeth. According to these proponents of scientific theories, former doctors did not accuse plaque or poor hygiene of tooth decay. Instead, they believed that small microscopic worms ate the teeth, and that sweet fruit was the cure to kill the worms. They did much more damage than medicine, fortunately, we now know better.

4. The earth is the only planet with water.

Because people look at the stars. We have always imagined what kind of life it is when it exists. Water is necessary for a life like ours. For so many people know, water is unique to the world. There is even evidence that Mars had running water on its surface. Later, as evidence, the scientists found rivers and lake beds on Mars.

This means that life on Mars may have been supported in the past. It was probably nothing but bacteria. However, some believe that a microphone still lives in frozen ice on the red planet. But we have not yet reached Mars, so we are not sure yet.

5.Human evolved from Neanderthals - false theories about science

It is a common misconception that humans are a more intelligent and intelligent evolutionary version of the Neanderthals. Although the evidence shows that it was untrue, we and Neanderthals lived at the same time. But even in different parts of the planet. There is ample evidence that Homo sapiens and Neanderthals breed to form the species we now call humans. The truth is that we are not a direct descendant of the Neanderthals, but a combination of the two gay sap races.

Passionate scientists always have unique ideas, but if they are too good to be true, they usually are. I hope you enjoyed the eight-fold list that scientists have found their old scientific theories wrong.

WHY IS SCIENCE WRONG SOMETIMES ?

Institutional problems in science

In my experience, scientists are largely slaves to their extraordinary curiosity and passion for research. The biggest advantage of a professor in his laboratory is that you can suggest and do research that interests you. Having your laboratory at one of the best research universities is extremely competitive inside and outside the job security institution ("right of residence") and beyond. institution (compete with other academics for research resources. limited funding).

With so many applications from highly qualified academics for faculty positions and scholarships, it is very beneficial to be able to demonstrate your skills and productivity. It is regularly judged based on a person's postal record. How long have you been in science? How many articles did you publish during this period? How high quality was this work, which usually depends on how often other researchers mention your work?

Because of this pressure to post a lot and show your success with a job, some aspects of the scientific process can be improved. I will focus on three of the most important points.

First, not many people are interested in publishing only replication studies and verifying someone else's results. Why? There is no fame in it. Few people mention the work; many journals do not even publish the study; there is no demonstration of the scientist's original and creative thinking. The whole time could be spent on another degree to have a better chance of a good career in academia. Repetition studies are important in science because they help to verify whether a result is a wave or that it is more likely to be true.

Second, we use statistics to conclude science. In rare cases, scientists collect data or hide it intentionally based on a diary. It is not common among academics and people who are taken at the end of their scientific careers. For most scientists, this is one of the most disgusting things you can do. A more common problem is that a statistical result is sometimes at the limit of what the community considered statistically significant. In these cases, slightly different statistical methods, which are also considered valid, lead to results that are on the "right" side of this limit. Since several analyzes are attempted, but only a few of them, the threshold for a conclusion is not reached by the researchers. Worse, those who choose to publish the result 'insignificantly' will often find that the magazines are not interested, or that their articles are not read in a magazine with minimal impact. This is called the "file loading problem" where trivial results end up in a closet somewhere and not in the world.

After all, I guess the amount you have to earn to get a good job is investing people too much in their ideas. If a good scientist posts a result and does not repeat it, they also post the replication error. They will change their minds about the best tests. However, it comes at a cost. This often makes the work of the past exhausting. The line of research that you may be trying to expand your career is beginning to crumble. The reason you made yourself famous in science and a hero to many is gone, and now you have to talk awkwardly about the reasons why you think you were wrong. It takes a lot of courage, but even more so when the atmosphere is so competitive.

There are real problems in science and, in a nutshell, I will talk about how to address some of these problems. However, before I do that, I want to talk about something that I believe is not a problem in the scientific institutions themselves, but that gives the public a distrust: sometimes the result of an experiment is not real.

The idea that some positive results are wrong is natural in statistics and taken for granted by the scientist, but not exactly intuitive. Scientists think in terms of evidence from many studies. They conclude the effects based on a consistent statistical threshold. This threshold means that if it does not, it is unlikely to have any effect. But it also means that we will not be so intense as not to have interesting effects when they exist.

Some areas have stricter thresholds than others. In physics, for example, there is often less controlled noise in an experiment than in psychology, where there are many other factors that can influence the effect. These stricter thresholds mean that physical outcomes are often more reliable than psychological outcomes. Psychology has not always chosen to publish unreliable results. Psychologists simply realize that many uncontrollable factors make noise about the effects they are interested in. That is why they have introduced a more liberal statistical portal to encourage progress in this area.

So instead of thinking in terms of scientific facts, scientists think in terms of useful models. Strong effects make them safer in the model, and the replication effect is more likely in other conditions. When there is very strong evidence and many retorts, different opinions usually come together for a "scientific consensus".

The media presents these studies, which contribute to the structure of the evidence, differently. Scientists need to interact with the public and share scientific progress. However, reporting on scientific evidence can be misleading as the context of the evidence is often not provided. The force of the scientific effect is bypassed. The amount of previous and sometimes conflicting research has been forgotten. Sometimes the media source draws conclusions that a scientist would never draw. The interpretation of the data at this point is often influenced by political thought. For example, one of my previous articles was about a study that was not mistakenly labeled a "victory" for equality movements.

The goal of the science writer is to add drama to a story so that more people can read it. The drama of dangerous climate change already exists; there is no need to become seasoned. But the article that gives preliminary evidence of ingredients in food that make resistance to eating more difficult is a bit boring and requires some work. What remains for us is a situation where it is difficult to distinguish "addictive cases like cocaine" because of the severity and scale of the evidence that "human effects on the climate are reaching dangerous levels".

WHAT IS A VIRUS?

Viruses are non-cellular microscopic infectious agents that can only replicate in a host cell. From a biological point of view, viruses cannot be classified as living from non-living organisms. This is because they certainly have properties of living organisms and non-living things.

In short, a virus is a non-cellular infectious entity made up of genetic material and proteins that can only be invaded and reproduced in the living cells of bacteria, plants, and animals.

For example, a virus cannot multiply outside the host. This is because viruses do not have the necessary cellular mechanism. It then enters and binds to a new host cell, injects its genetic material, reproduces using the host's genetic material, and eventually divides the host cell and releases the new virus.

Viruses can also crystallize, which no other living organism can do. It is these factors that determine the classification of viruses in the gray zone, both living and non-living.

STRUCTURE AND FUNCTION OF VIRUSES

The viruses are small and smaller in size and range between 30-50 nm. They usually do not have a cell wall, but are surrounded by a protective protein coating called the capsule. It can be considered a genetic trait and is characterized by the combined development of the virus and the host. It contains RNA or DNA as the genetic material

Viruses are primarily dependent on a host that provides complex metabolic machinery of prokaryotic or eukaryotic cells for reproduction. The main task of the virus is to deliver its DNA or RNA genome into the host cell, which can then be transcribed by the host cell. The viral genome is packaged in a circulating symmetrical protein. The nucleic acid-associated protein (also known as a nucleoproprotein) produces the nucleoside with the genome.

ARE VIRUSES ALIVE?

Viruses are, in a sense, living and non-living. They have genetic information that comes from natural selection. They come together. You can say nothing about rocks, clouds or stars. However, they do not have an internal chemical process to sustain life, such as growth, reproduction, or adaptation to their environment. In this way, they are almost as inert as non-living matter. So, what is it? Many scientists believe that they are a precursor to life, a form of pre-life that gives us an idea of how life evolved from organizing and self-replicating organic molecules. Others believe that they are more like seeds with life potential if they find the right environment (a cellular host). Still, others consider them parasites, pieces of genes that escape from a previous host. This question has therefore not yet been fully answered, but the search for the answer has led to many fascinating discoveries.

IS VIRUS A LIVING ORGANISM ?

Most people assume that there is a live virus of some kind. We usually give viruses the same mental category as bacteria - a category we often call 'bacteria'. We believe that all bacteria are the same because we consider them to be microscopic organisms that cause disease. We try to avoid exposure to bacteria and rely on vaccines and medicines to protect them. However, this simple concept surpasses almost everything interesting around viruses and bacteria. It especially ignores the fact that viruses and bacteria are completely different things - just as different as day and night. An important difference is that bacteria are living things, but not viruses.

This is, of course, an anti-intuitive idea. How on earth can a virus not live? We know that viruses - or at least some types of viruses can make people sick, just as certain types of bacteria can make us sick. In both cases, the microscopic objects enter our body and multiply rapidly. If a virus is not a living thing, then how can it be? Why are bacteria not considered alive as the virus?

Let's first look at the properties of the bacterium to find out why bacteria are considered living. Bacteria are mostly cells. All bacteria are living cells, whole. On the outside is a porous cell wall that provides stiffness and determines the shape of the bacterium. Inside is a plasma membrane, a thin layer that maintains the cell and separates the cell contents from the rest of the world. We sometimes refer to the cell contents - anything in the plasma membrane - as refractory plasma. However, this shadow expression means little. The cell content consists of many different substances - proteins, fats, carbohydrates, DNA, water, and so on. The cell almost always undergoes a large number of biochemical processes, and it is these ongoing processes, all under the indirect control of the DNA of the cell, that cause the cell to "survive".

Because a bacterium is alive, it can kill. Anything that

permanently disrupts the ongoing biochemical processes kills the cell. For example, too hot or too cold temperatures can kill it. Toxic compounds can kill them. A tear kills the plasma membrane that opens it. And because the cell is alive, it can also die. The biochemical processes that take place in the cell require energy. If the cell no longer has energy - and if the cell can not replace the energy to eat suitable food, the cell dies.

Although bacteria are unicellular beings, their cells are smaller and simpler than human cells. Bacterial cells are much simpler than the cells in other living things - even the cells of other unicellular organisms. Therefore, they stand on their own as the simplest kind of living organism in modern biological classification systems. (For more information on classifying living things, see my previous article "How Many Kinds of Living Things Are There?")

Although a plasma membrane separates bacteria from the outside world, the membrane must be selectively permeable for the bacteria to survive. (This property can be temporarily suspended in certain bacteria that become inactive in the form of strongly persistent endospores.) Food, water, and other nutrients must be able to enter the bacterial cell through the membrane and waste products must escape from the cell.

Viruses are very different from bacteria. The virus usually contains only a fragment of DNA or RNA wrapped in a protective protein layer. (Some viruses contain a little more but not much more.) Just as a bacterial cell is much smaller and simpler than a human cell, a virus is much smaller and simpler than a bacterium. Viruses have no protoplasm. It does not have a plasma membrane. It has no continuous metabolic processes. He does not eat food. No waste is sent. He can not be hungry. Unlike bacteria, a virus cannot reproduce on its own. Until a virus hits a suitable host cell, it remains a completely inert particle without the essential properties we associate with living humans - except for the fragment of DNA or RNA.

(Note: RNA has the same information as DNA, but in a normal cell the permanent copy of the genetic code is stored as DNA, and RNA is usually used to make temporary working copies of parts of the code.)

However, a virus has two very important properties that make it extremely powerful:

1) The protein coat can adhere to suitable host cells, after which the viral DNA or RNA enters the cell.

2) Invasive DNA or RNA redirects the metabolic activities of the abducted cell and converts the cell into a factory to remove many other viral particles.

Therefore, viruses are just random pieces of genetic material - they are pieces of genetic material that can kidnap living cells. The virus does not have to have all the genetic information needed to make the hijacked cell function. It only needs enough DNA or RNA to reverse the cell's activities. It can be compared to modern pirates kidnapping an oil tanker. Pirates can approach the giant oil tanker on a small motorboat. Once onboard the tanker, private individuals do not have to know the details of the ship's management - they only have to force the captain and crew to keep their orders. Similarly, the DNA or RNA in the virus takes over the set cell, but some of the cell's original DNA may still be needed to make the cell function.

Now that the hijacked cell mechanism has been redirected to produce more virus particles, the newly created viruses need a way to escape to infect other cells. In some viral diseases, viruses do not even escape from the host cell before the cell is filled with new virus particles, at which point the cell breaks down and kills the cell, but it releases much of the virus. In other viral diseases, new viruses can germinate because the cell produces more and more virus particles.

Let's now look at the biggest differences between a bacterium and a virus. A bacterium is a small living thing that consists of a simple living cell. Because it is alive, it consumes energy and therefore needs food energy to stay alive. Bacteria have innumerable ways of making money, namely feeding, evolving food, and only a small fraction of bacterial species cause disease. A healthy bacterium can reproduce by dividing it into two parts. In contrast, viruses do not survive - they are essentially unwanted pieces of DNA or RNA. A viral particle is completely inert until it abducts a suitable host cell. The only way a virus can reproduce - or do anything - is to kidnap a live cell from a sensitive species.

Since all viruses live their lives by abducting living cells, it can be said that all viruses are harmful. However, ignore an important point. Each virus type has a specific host species - or a set of host species that have a connection - to infect and abduct the corresponding cells. There are many types of viruses that are completely harmless to humans, although it harms some other types. How should we think of a virus that attacks bacteria that cause diseases in humans? The presence of the virus can even help us protect against bacterial diseases. It can be said that the enemy of my enemy is my friend. The same goes for any other virus that attacks parasites, or for that matter all bacteria that attack parasites. For example, we use pesticides to control various pests that affect our crops.

Even though viruses do not exist and have no place in the taxonomy of living things, we often include viruses when we talk about 'microorganisms'. Since all other organisms live, this survey is misleading, although it makes sense in many other ways. This is especially true when we talk about "pathogenic microorganisms", also known as pathogens. The word "pathogen" originally meant everything that caused a disease, but now the term is usually limited to microorganisms. In addition to viruses and bacteria, human diseases can be caused by many other categories of infectious agents, although we refer to most of them as parasites rather than pathogens or "germs". Malaria, for example, is caused by a microscopic protozoan and not a virus or bacterium, which causes nearly a million deaths each year.

If a virus does not live, then does it make sense to talk about 'killing a virus'? Strictly speaking, a virus cannot be killed, but a virus can be destroyed and is the same for all practical purposes. One can therefore argue that there is no harm or confusion in talking about killing a virus. However, such terminology can lead to misunderstandings. It is much more difficult to find effective antiviral drugs than the invention of antibacterial agents (called antibiotics), precisely because the virus particles are not alive. This significantly reduces the possibility of attacking the virus. It should also be noted that antibiotics - designed to attack bacteria - are completely ineffective against viral diseases. So you can not cure colds by taking antibiotics.

This begs the question: what common diseases are caused by viruses and what bacteria do they cause? Known viral diseases include colds, flu, measles, HIV / Aids, herpes, mumps, measles, rubella, shale, viral hepatitis (type A) rabies, polio, West Nile, dengue, yellow fever, and ebola. Known bacterial diseases include cholera, tuberculosis, typhus, tetanus, Lyme disease, chlamydia, salmonellosis, syphilis, diphtheria, leprosy, abdominal plague, whooping cough, listeriosis, psittacosis, rheumatic fever, scarlet fever, anthrax, and throat.

In recent years, the science of drug discovery for the treatment of certain types of viral diseases has made significant progress. However, because viral diseases are often so difficult to cure, most emphasis in the past has been on vaccines, which can not only cure the disease but also help prevent it. Vaccines work by training the body to recognize and attack certain types of viruses early in the infection before the viral infection gets out of control.

On the contrary, we have a wide range of antibiotics that have been effective (or were previously effective) against a wide range of bacterial diseases. Unfortunately, the more we use a specific antibiotic, the greater the chance that we will breed strains of antibiotic-resistant diseases. Therefore, measured over many years, each commonly used antibiotic usually has a useful life, often shorter than the typical human life. Another problem with antibiotics is that they kill the "good" bacteria along with the bad bacteria. There are many types of bacteria, most of which do not cause disease. Many bacteria are very useful to us, especially some of the bacteria that live in the gut.

After all, a virus is not a living thing - and in fact, it is only a piece of illegally copied genetic material (DNA or RNA). However, because of its ability to participate in the biological processes of a living cell, a virus acts like a living being after being abducted by the cell. For primarily practical purposes, it makes sense to pinch viruses with pathogenic bacteria when discussing ways to prevent diseases spread by microorganisms. However, because viruses do not live - and also because they are very small - we face more barriers to controlling virus-related diseases than are caused by bacteria.

Viruses were difficult to classify, with some researchers claiming that they did not contain live DNA and RNA, but new research shows that they not only lived long enough but that they also preceded the first modern cells.

Viruses have just been planted on the tree of life and are located in the oldest place at the foot of the tree. They are not so-called "animals, vegetables or minerals", but occur in their own unique group.

It's just an atypical lifestyle that's a little different from ours.

They are not completely independent. Instead, they move in and out of our bodies, stealing resources, and producing their offspring. In short, we need to expand on how we define life and the activities that go along with it. "

Studying viruses is challenging because the sequences encoding their genomes can change rapidly. Consequently, the researchers chose to name a fold - the structural building blocks of proteins that give proteins their complex, three-dimensional shapes.

The researchers compared folded structures across different branches of the tree of life and wrote an evolutionary history of the folds and organisms from which the genome was coded. The researchers did this for 5,080 organisms that showed all branches of the tree of life, including 3,460 viruses.

They identified 442 protein folds shared between cells and viruses and 66 unique to viruses.

Viruses undergo more lifestyle tests

The researchers theorize that viruses evolved at a time when primary cells express genetic material, which can then be acquired by viruses. Most viruses then acquired the ability to surround themselves in the protective protein coatings, capsules, which over time became more advanced. Capsids cause viruses to become infected in previously infected cells.

Viruses can be "depicted as cells that have lost and lost genetic material to compensate for the benefits of their interaction with other cells."

Viruses are likely to produce their own new genes, and some viruses are giant. On the smaller end of the spectrum, there are Ebola-like viruses that have only seven genes. At the extreme end, mimivirus has recently been discovered whose genome is the same size or larger than parasitic bacteria.

Viruses get their own immune system. When viruses that attack bacteria take up an 'immune system', they can disarm the host cell, and then they can continue the infection and kill the host cell.

Such a study of viruses enables researchers to better understand the life cycle and evolution of these devices with a view to future treatment of viruses with more targeted and effective approaches.

At least the researchers hope that the argument that viruses do not live on their own is dead.

As confirmed, there are viruses.

Rarely has anyone looked at a potentially deadly infectious disease and exclaimed, 'This is a beauty'. However, the sculptor removed bacteria and viruses from their invisible world and placed them in our own country.

HOW DO VIRUS REPRODUCE

Viruses can only reproduce once they have found a host cell. There are some viruses in the air, such as flu and cold viruses: they can infect the host through the nose and mouth. Some viruses can only be ingested or injected into the host through hypothermic injection, sexual intercourse or through things like kissing. Here are how viruses can reproduce.

Viruses go through a multi-phase life cycle. The virus first binds to the host via specific proteins on the cell surface. These proteins are usually receptors that differ depending on the type of virus affecting the cell. Once the virus is attacked, the cell enters through endocytosis or fusion. Host mechanisms are used to replicate viral DNA or RNA and essential proteins. After these new viruses become obsolete, the host is compiled so that the new viruses can repeat the cycle.

An additional pre-replication phase, known as the lysogenic or dormant phase, occurs only in a certain number of viruses. During this stage, the virus can remain in the host for long periods without making any noticeable changes to the host host. Once activated, these viruses can immediately enter the lytic phase, where they can replicate, mature and release. For example, HIV can remain inactive for ten years.

Viruses can infect bacterial and eukaryotic cells. Animal viruses are the most well-known eukaryotic viruses, but they can also infect plant viruses. These plant viruses usually need the help of insects or bacteria to enter the cell wall of a plant. If the plant becomes infected, the virus can kill various diseases that usually do not kill the plant but disrupt the growth and development of the plant.

A virus that infects bacteria is called a bacterium or phage. Bacteriophages have the same lifespan as eukaryotic viruses and can infect and destroy bacteria by lysis. These viruses are replicating so efficiently that entire bacterial colonies can be quickly destroyed. Bacteriophages are used to diagnose and treat infections with bacteria such as E. coli and Salmonella.

1. Lithic cycle

In this cycle, the virus reproduces after infusion from the human host cell with its nucleic acid. It uses the protein layer of the host cell for reproduction. These reproductive virus cells continue to increase until they explode the host cell. They then move on to another fresh host cell and the cycle continues.

2. Lysogenic cycle

Viruses that take longer use this cycle to reproduce for reproduction - this is the case with viruses such as the herpes virus and the HIV virus. During this cycle, the nucleic acid of the virus takes time to develop full attachment to the host cell. This happens because the nucleic acid in such viruses is not active but eventually starts the replication process and destroys the host cell.

WHAT'S STORM?

A thunderstorm is an episode of bad weather negative and a serious location of the atmosphere. Storms can be very diverse, where the products and the greatest seriousness are there. And thunderstorms can be fewer colors end and time or blouse end and week. It can only affect square kilometers or thousands. Some storms are harmless and others catastrophic. The size and strength of a storm depending on the amount of energy in the atmosphere. Greater research into temperature and atmosphere is trying to lead to the bigger storm. Types of storms use storms, tornadoes, hurricanes, and winter storms such as snowstorms.

What casuses storm?

Storm surges, the temporary rise in sea levels during a storm, are dangerous when the storm - usually a hurricane or other tropical storm - hits the land. Water can spread everywhere except on land as the storm moves to the coast, which can cause flooding to the coast and other forms of hurricane damage. The force of waves and currents, for example, can lead to soil erosion and the destruction of buildings. Seawater that ends up in lakes, streams, and aquifers is dangerous to aquatic life and drinking water.

A storm is essentially a natural disaster that causes any change in the atmosphere, whether it is a change in pressure, temperature, or water level. Strong winds usually have heavy rainfall, which can cause destruction.

Storms occur when an air pressure system is surrounded by a high-pressure air system.

Both air systems create very variable winds under varying pressure and create thunderclouds that can cause heavy rain.

Storm waves are changes in the water level that create atmospheric force. especially due to the wind pressure at sea level and due to the fluctuations in the atmospheric surface pressure associated with storms. It lasts several hours to 2 or 3 days and has a large spatial scale concerning the water depth. In extreme cases, they can raise or lower the water level by a few meters. An increase in the level referred to as a 'positive' increase and a decrease as a 'negative' increase. The storm waves overlap normal astronomical tides, creating fluctuations in the severity of the moon and sun. The storm component can come from a time series of sea levels recorded with a tidal meter

The term 'storm surge' is sometimes used to refer to the sea level (including the tidal component) during a storm. It is important to be aware of the use of the term and what it means to avoid confusion. Storms also create surface wind waves with periods of seconds and wavelengths abroad that are equal to or less than the water depth.

Positive storm surges combined with tidal and wind waves can lead to coastal flooding, possibly the most destructive natural danger of geophysical origin in terms of deaths and damage. If the tidal range is large, the timing of the high tide is critical to the high tide and a large wave can occur at low tide. Negative waves reduce the water depth and can endanger navigation. Associated storm surges, overflowing tides and wave-generated currents can lead to extreme currents and soils responsible for coastal erosion. A correct understanding of storm surges, the ability to predict them, and measures to reduce their devastating consequences are therefore important issues.

Types of storm and classification of existence

Rain storm

If the rainfall falls for a very long time and snow accumulates on so-called exposed surfaces, it is called ice storms. When rain freezes in the air, it reaches the ground in the form of a vacuum. Sleet is a mixture of snow and rain, but very transparent, unlike snow. It usually starts with snow and ends with icy rain before the impact. People usually think of them as a light rain that occurs under low normal temperatures.

Hail storm

Storm clouds form hailstones when the rain they produce freezes before hitting the ground. When the wind is drawn, the icy rain hangs until it is too heavy to handle and hits the ground in the form of hailstones.

Bloodstorms are precipitation in the form of solid ice. The pieces of ice that fall to the ground are called hailstones. They are irregular in shape and perpendicular to the spherical shape. Larger hailstones have low onions ranging from clear ice to opaque ice. Serious warnings are issued when hailstones reach alarming sizes.

Blizzard

Severe storms are caused by heavy snow. Although not as dangerous as ice storms, they pose secondary dangers in the form of kites. Blizzard needs a lot of external humidity. The converging air in the center of the system must have an outlet to move to interfaces to continue this cycle.

Windstorm

A storm with strong winds and no precipitation is called a storm. A short, severe storm accompanied by rain is called a 'scream'. On the other hand, a violent storm of air, snow or hail is called a 'storm'.

Sand storm

A sandstorm is a large storm surge that forms in dry places, and a sandstorm usually occurs in the desert when dust particles are blown over long distances. Dust storms or sandstorms are common in arid regions. They originate in an area with little agriculture or drought. A sandstorm usually starts within minutes and blows for days on end.

Thunder

Thunderstorms and lightning are characterized by thunderstorms. Hurricanes are hailstorms that cause hail. It is common in the tropics.

A clear gale is a clear sign of a dark sky with clouds rising in the form of a rapidly rising precipitation.

There are four types of storms: unicellular storms, multicellular storms, multicellular clusters, and supercellular storms. Single thunderstorms are storms of impulses. As with all thunderstorms, it also forms areas with high humidity. It takes less than an hour, but can cause heavy hail and severe tornadoes.

Multicellular thunderstorms are a group of unicellular thunderstorms in different phases of life. It makes everyone aware of their presence in case of lightning. Multicellular line storms consist of a forward scallop line. Multicellular storms can cause medium-sized hail, flash floods and weak tornadoes.

Fire Storm

A firestorm occurs when a hell that causes intense flames catches the air around and ignites the flames in the middle of the storm.

The pull out of the storm absorbs oxygen and increases combustion, which increases heat production.

Burning or shaking leaves to ashes is a clear sign of a distant storm.

If there is a firestorm on it, it burns in isolated firestorms and weak tornadoes.

Hurricane

A tropical cyclone is used to describe windstorms that occur over tropical or subtropical waters. When a tropical cyclone reaches prolonged winds of more than 85 miles per hour, it is classified as a hurricane, typhoon or cyclone, depending on where the storm is coming from. A hurricane turns left and a cyclone rotates clockwise.

It is called a 'cyclone' in the Indian Ocean and the South Pacific Ocean and a typhoon in the West Pacific Ocean. A hurricane loses power when it comes to landing because the moisture it receives is removed from the sea. While many people view the storm as a storm, it is the damage that causes the most damage.

Tornadoes

Tornadoes are a clockwise column that rotates clockwise. They are called "spinners". Tornadoes have narrow points that touch the ground and are usually accompanied by dirt and dust. The water drain is related to a tornado over the water. While a dust devil is often mistaken for a tornado, it is a slight improvement in the rising air that collects small particles of dust and debris.

A tornado forms even after a strong storm. Tornadoes usually move from southwest to northeast. But it is incredible and can usually switch roads at the last minute. There are 5 steps: warning, warning, bell, warning and tornado. A tornado is usually accompanied by strong winds and lightning.

The making and existence of a storm

Happened what happened in the atmosphere that caused this violent storm? Weather conditions in summer and winter were hit by extreme forces. The main difference between a tropical cyclone is also called a hurricane, and a winter cyclone is the energy source. A tropical cyclone draws heat from the ocean and rises to release that heat into the atmosphere near the center of the storm. In contrast, winter storms get most of their energy from temperature contrasts in the atmosphere, and this energy is usually distributed over greater distances.

Sandy started out as a classic hurricane, drawing energy from the warm waters of the Caribbean and moving north along the Gulf Stream. Sandy then made a sharp left on the shores of New Jersey and New York and encountered a winter storm system.

When the power source Sandy switched from warm ocean water to the atmosphere, it turned into a winter cyclone and grew significantly. High winds stretched 1,000 miles, bringing waves to coastal areas and flowering conditions in the mountains. Tunnels were turned into rivers and parking lots into ponds. Residents returned to see their belongings floating in puddles of water in their homes and backyards. Cars pushed around as toys and sandy mountains filled the streets. The results lasted days, weeks, and in some places even months. A neighborhood had even been destroyed on the ground.

The life circle of a thunder storm

The three main components of storm growth and development are instability, humidity, and an upliftment mechanism, which have been discussed in previous topics. The following information explains how a thunderstorm will develop when all of these ingredients are available.

If the storm is not severe, three phases are activated: Cumulus, adults, and distribution. In the first phase (cumulus) we see how the cloud develops and grows into thunderstorms due to the increase in temperature (or the realization). The side effect of the air begins to cool and subside as it rises, and in the event of a thunderstorm, it can raise thousands upon thousands of feet before finally stopping! During this phase, small raindrops may form and try to fall; However, the wind flow in the update could push raindrops higher into the cloud, instead of letting it out. Raindrops collide at this level and accumulate in larger droplets due to the abrasive turbulence in the cloud.

Eventually, the raindrops become large and heavy enough to fall from the cloud to the ground. This is the beginning of the second phase (for adults). The term subtraction is used to describe rain and fresh air that begins to sink after a storm. Think of refuge as a fresh air bubble in the cloud moving toward the earth's surface (rather than an updated design). Due to a decrease, the temperature in an area can change quickly in a short time.

As the pulldown hits the ground, it begins to spread in all directions. In this case, a gust of wind may form. The eruption is actually a barrier that separates the cooling rain air from the hot environmentalists, as shown in Figure C. Sometimes a cloud creates a threatening platform or cloud that rolls along the stroke. As you can imagine, the wind behind the wind can be very strong and sometimes even reach difficult levels.

The life cycle of hail Storm

Hail comes from small droplets with a diameter of 0.02 mm. Once large masses of these droplets are updated, they reach heights colder than the surface. Due to their fast behavior and the lack of iron cores in their path, they cool below $0\,^{\circ}C$ without freezing (supercooling.)

Soon they will be further cooled in ice particles. After this change in density, they can enter the atmospheric tunnel created by the upgrade and collect supercooled cloud droplets. If these growth conditions persist, the core layers and ice droplets can reach between one and five millimeters in diameter. This new construction has a small snowball texture, called a group.

Extraction can revive the grain by cooling cooler drops and ice particles and then starting the exercise cycle again. The risk of collision and assimilation of ice particles increases exponentially. By applying supercooled droplets and depositing ice particles, hailstones can form the size of the beads or more, depending on the strength and length of their updates and wind directions created on their own. training. These remarkable hailstones have now become large enough to be struck and coupled with other hailstones; and with the help of increasingly common cooled droplets, they can freeze enough to stay close until they reach the surface.

Hail can take many sizes and shapes. Depending on the environmental conditions during its formation, it can appear almost spherical, pointed, lenticular, or irregular. In addition to the presence of ice cores and cloud droplets, and the presence of vertically oriented wind, the electromagnetic force is involved in the formation of hailstones, as seen in cross-sections.

The life circle of a lightning storm

Lightning is an electric shock caused by imbalances between storm clouds and the ground or within the clouds themselves. Most lightning occurs in clouds.

'Leaf flash' describes a lightning bolt that illuminates an entire cloud base. Other visible bolts may appear as beads, ribbons, or rocket bolts.

During a storm, particles of rain, ice, or snow that collide in thunder clouds increase the imbalance between storm clouds and the ground and often charge the lower parts of the clouds negatively after the storm. Objects on the ground, such as church muscles, trees, and the earth itself, are positively charged, creating an imbalance that nature seeks to correct by passing electricity between the two charges.

Lightning is extremely hot: lightning can heat the surrounding air to five times hotter than the surface of the sun. This heat causes the surrounding air to expand and vibrate rapidly, creating the crackling thunder we hear shortly after the lightning bolt.

The life circle of an Hurricane

A tropical storm becomes a hurricane when the heat and humidity of the ocean during a low-pressure system combined with light winds near the sea surface.

Light winds are sucked into the system and begin to swing clockwise. As the storm progresses, it collects more moisture and releases more heat, allowing the hurricane to continue.

When it reaches a sustained wind of 74 km / h and forms a circular pattern of clouds that continues to grow as it moves across the ocean. It is now a well-developed hurricane with all three components; the rain bands, the eyeball, and the eye of the pendulum.

The hurricane will continue to grow in size and strength as it crosses the ocean and will collect more moisture and heat as it moves. A strong, well-organized hurricane can "survive" more than two weeks at sea if conditions remain favorable.

DEFINITION OF CRYSTAL

A crystal is a material formed by the arrangement of atoms, molecules, or ions. The grid extends in three dimensions.

Since there are repeating devices, the crystals have identifiable structures. Large crystals show equal distances (faces) and well-defined angles.

Crystals with clear planes are called cathedral crystals, while crystals without defined planes are called cathedral crystals. Crystals that consist of ordered atomic matrices that are not always periodic are called quasi-crystals.

How Crystals Are Formed

The crystal formation process is called crystallization. Crystallization occurs frequently when solid crystals grow from a liquid of solution.

When a hot solution cools or when a saturated solution disappears, the particles come close enough to form chemical bonds. Crystals can also represent the word by a direct shutdown from the gas phase. The particles are organized like solid crystals in a way that is organized by liquid crystals but can flow

Types of chrystals shape : shapes and structures

Crystals refer to any solid whose components such as atoms, ions or molecules are arranged or arranged in a repeating pattern in all directions. Cryptography involves the scientific study of crystals and their formation, and crystallization or solidification is defined as crystal formation.

Types of crystals

There are two common methods and methods for classifying crystals. One method is to group them according to their structure and the other groups based on their physical and chemical properties.

Group by shape

Seven types of crystals fall under this classification. are:

Isometric or cubic

This type is not always a cube. This type contains octahedron and dodecahedron.

Hexagonal

This type of crystal is a six-sided prism. This type of diameter creates a hexagon.

Tetragonal

This crystal looks almost like a cubic crystal, but one is further back than the other, leading to the formation of double pyramids and prisms.

Triclinic

This crystal is not symmetrical from measurement to side, therefore different types of shapes are created.

Monoclinic

This type determines the formation of double prisons and pyramids and has the appearance of complex tetrogonal crystals.

orthorhombic

This crystal is a double prism or a pyramid with a diamond as a base in cross-section.

How do crystals grow?

Crystals or minerals can be found everywhere in our area. How did they bloom? How did it happen? How fast are they growing?

Such crystals occur in nature, and chalcanthite is the name of a mineral. It is often crystallized in copper mines from groundwater. They are formed at ambient temperatures, perhaps 10 ° C, and perfect crystals are formed as they grow very slowly.

Another crystal that grows at ambient temperatures in nature is gypsum (also known as selenite), the hydrated calcium sulfate. In dry salt lakes, you can find clear transparent gypsum crystals that are three feet long, or a rosette group of coated crystals known as a "desert rose". If the lake is watered, salts may have dissolved. During evaporation during the drought, when the saturated water arrives, the salts first crystallize gypsum and then salt or halite blocks and other salts, possibly even gold nuggets.

Quartz is the most common mineral you can find. It forms a multitude of single crystals (eg rock crystals and amethyst), crystal aggregates, and microcrystalline decorative materials such as agate, carnelian, and jasper. Quartz is found in large crystalline rocks such as quartz and granite. Calcite is another common mineral found in temperate crystals in small and microscopic crystals in spheres, limestone and as shells and fossils, and as white veins traversing sedimentary rocks.

Here are some different crystal growth processes that occur in nature, using common examples:

(1) Slow cooling by melting, such as. B. Silicate Magma, d. H. Lava flows from a volcano, starts temperature around 1200 ° C, and rapid cooling (days or weeks) produces volcanic rock with very small crystals of feldspar, quartz or olivine, etc. A fraction of a millimeter in size. In contrast, granite magma cools slowly from about 700 ° C below the earth's surface, producing coarse crystals from 1 to 10 mm in size of quartz, feldspar, and mica, which can last for thousands of years.

(2) The growth of crystals from a saturated aqueous solution by allowing the solvent, which is water, to cool or evaporate or by transferring components on a temperature gradient. Temperatures can range from environmental conditions up to 600 degrees Celsius and the crystallization of the granite-linked pegmatite veins.

(3) Growth of crystals from steam or steam for a solid reaction. Often use water vapor to form ice crystals such as frost and icy window races. Volcanic holes, which emit foul-smelling gases, can cause the environment to develop a yellow shell and more sulfur crystals to grow directly from the sulfur vapor. Also the formation of 'dry ice' (solid carbon dioxide microcrystals) on the surface of Mars, the steaming process by which artificial diamonds are forged.

(4) Growing biological crystals: Many living things can grow microscopic crystals that are an integral part of their body. Animals and fish have bones and teeth, shellfish or polygonaragonite have calcite scales, small forests use silica, all of which are carried out at constant ambient temperature. Life forms are very clever!

(5) Recrystallization from very small to smaller to larger crystals, often at a constant temperature. The medium can be melted (high temperature), or an aqueous solution or steam. The driving force here is the difference in surface energy. A given microcrystalline weight has a much larger surface area than an equivalent single crystal of the same weight. A lower energy state of the system is obtained by spontaneous decomposition of the microcrystals and less growth (ideally one). Very common in nature.

From a geological point of view, limestone or limestone from small calcite or aragonite scales can recrystallize from much larger calcite crystals if buried deep in the earth's crust. Sedimentary sediments consisting of small clay and other alternative crystal particles can make them more stable than the original. Hence we have the metamorphic sequence from mudstone with slate or slate to mica lath and gneiss, which is formed with increasing temperature and temperature.

(6) Solidarity reactions or crystal growth within the solid phase. A good example is dissolving glass, whether it is natural (lava obsidian or artifacts) or man-made glasses. Glasses are usually formed by rapidly cooling the silicate melt so that crystals did not have time to germinate and grow. Glasses (even window glass) given on time will be ready at some point, maybe 1,000 or a million years later.

After all, the phenomenon of crystal growth and the opposite of the crystal solution surrounds us all the time. The driving force is to achieve a lower energy state for a given system. We live in a heterogeneity of overlapping systems, each doing its own thing. The change in nature is extremely slow and is rarely noticed until you experiment with the growth of alum or copper sulphate crystals in your kitchen or workshop ...

HOW HUMAN HAVE JUDGED LIFE AND HER EXISTENCE

It is common to denounce modern science because they do not make value judgments. It is said that a living and functioning man has no value for freedom; he needs to know what to aim for. If science does not answer this question, it is sterile. However, the objection is unfounded. Science does not add value but gives the employee all the information he needs regarding his assessments. It is only silent when asked if it is worth living alone.

This issue has, of course, been raised and will continue to be addressed. What is the point of all these human efforts and activities if no one can finally escape death and humiliation? A man lives in the shadow of death. Whatever he accomplishes on his pilgrimage, he must one day die, leaving behind everything he has built. Any moment can end. Only one thing is certain about the future of the individual: death. As for this inevitable end result, any human effort seems meaningless and meaningless.

In addition, human actions should be considered crazy, even if they are judged only on their immediate goals. He can never give complete satisfaction; Only a moment is allowed to partially eliminate the error. Once a will is fulfilled, new desires arise and they seek satisfaction. Civilization is said to influence poor people because it multiplies their desires and does not diminish but teeth. The busy actions and actions of every busy man, their pulley, pressure, and pressure are not specified because it does not bring happiness or peace. Peace of mind and peace of mind can not be achieved through worldly action and ambition but through resignation and resignation. The only behavior suitable for the wise is to escape to the inactivity of life, which is only meditative.

But the power of human life energy is subject to an irresistible force subject to all this regret, doubt, and scrubbing. Man cannot escape death. But now he lives; and life, not death, takes hold of it. Whatever happens to him in the future, he can not work the need for hours. As long as a man survives, he can not help but succumb to the cardinal impulse, the important momentum. It is the innate nature of man that he tries to preserve and strengthen his life, that he is dissatisfied and that he wants to create unrest, that he strives for what is called happiness. A useless and unacceptable ID works in any life. This identity is the implication of all the implications, the power that drives a man in life and action, the original and disorderly desire for a fuller and happier life. It works as long as a man lives and he just stops aging.

Human reason serves this important tendency. The biological function of the soil is to sustain and promote life and to delay its extraction as much as possible. Thought and action do not contradict nature; On the contrary, they are the most important aspects of human nature. The most accurate description of the man is how he differs from non-human beings: a functioning warrior against forces unfavorable to his life.

One can therefore speak freely of the primacy of irrational elements. If our life in the universe cannot be explained, analyzed, or imagined, there is still a narrow field in which man can take away the turmoil to a certain extent. Here you will find advice on common sense and rationality, science, and functional action. Neither the limited results nor the small results a man can achieve there indicate radical resignation and inertia. No philosophical prejudice can ever prevent a healthy person from taking actions that he says meet his needs. It may be true that there is a desire for rest and inactivity that disturbs only vegetation but in the deepest recesses of the human soul. But in the living person, whatever they are, these desires are balanced by the urge to act and improve their own condition. As soon as the powers of dismissal reign, a man dies; it does not turn into a plant.

Practice and the economy do not tell someone whether they should give up life or give up. Life itself is a purpose in itself and the unknown forces that flow from it and are set on fire and thus from the light of man

Economic and valuable sentences

While many people blame the economy for its neutrality in terms of value judgments, others owe their indifference to them. Some argue that economics should convey valuations and therefore are not really scientific because the criterion of science is to ignore the value. Others argue that a good economy must and can be impartial and that only bad economists sin against this intervention.

The semantic confusion in discussing the issues is due to the inaccurate use of the terms by many economists. An economist examines whether the result of a measure can be the result of p, and is advised to obtain it, and finds that the result of p, but g, is not an effect that even proponents of the measure consider undesirable not. If this economist pronounces the result of his study and says that it is a bad deed, then he is not judging any value. It exposes that the measure is not suitable for those who want to achieve a goal. In this sense, free trade economists attacked the defense. They have shown that the protection does not increase as their masters believe, but lowers the total quantity of products and therefore those who prefer to see a product enhancer as a smaller product. In this sense, economists criticize policies in terms of the goals they want to achieve.

When an economist mentions a bad minimum wage policy, it means that its consequences are contrary to the purpose of those who advocate its implementation.

From the same perspective, practice and economics look at the basic principle of human and social development, i.e. cooperation in the social division of labor is a more effective way of trading than the autonomous isolation of individuals. Praxeology and economics do not say that men should work together peacefully within social ties; they simply say that men should act in this way if they want their actions to be more successful than usual. Adherence to the moral rules necessary to establish, maintain and strengthen social cooperation is not seen as a sacrifice for a mythical entity, but as the use of the most effective way of acting as a price to pay word. pay. used to obtain higher-value results.

The united forces of schools and anti-liberal dogmatism are opposed to the autonomous, rational and voluntary replacement of the heterogeneous doctrines of intuitionism and the commands of dissemination. his description and analysis of human nature and the main sources of human activities. There is no need to add more to the return of this critique that every page in this book offers. It is only necessary to repeat one point, because on the one hand it is the teaching of every modern imitation player, and on the other hand it offers a good excuse for the general intellectuals to examine economic studies carefully.

In the preconceived ideas, the economy assumes that rationalization is aimed solely or primarily at the material well-being of people. But in reality, men prefer irrational goals over rational goals. They control the urge to realize myths and ideals more than the urge to enjoy a higher standard of living.

HOW ECONOMY AFFECTS HUMAN LIFE

The economy does not accept or accept that men only or primarily aim for what is known as substantial well-being. Economics as a branch of the more general theory of human action deals with all human actions, e.g. the intentional goal of man to achieve the chosen goals, regardless of the goals. It does not make sense to apply a rational or irrational concept to the chosen end goals. We can call the latter data irrational, .i. the things that our thinking cannot analyze or diminish to other things that are ultimately given. Then the end goal one chooses is irrational. It is no more rational or less focused on wealth like Croesus than on poverty like a Buddhist monk.

What these critics consider when using the term rational end is the desire for material well-being and a higher standard of living. The point is to know if their claims are true that men in general, and our contemporaries in particular, are driven by a desire to realize myths and dreams rather than a desire to improve their material well-being. Although no smart person can give the right answer, we can ignore the problem. Because the economy does not speak against or against mites. It is completely neutral towards the doctrine of syndicalism, the doctrine of credit extension, and all these doctrines, as it can present itself as myths and support their myths of their partners. These promotions are only a problem in that they are considered as a suitable way to achieve certain goals. Business does not say that the Union is a bad myth. He simply explains that raising the wage rate is an inadequate way for anyone trying to make money. It is up to everyone to decide whether it is more important to dispel the union myth than to avoid the inevitable consequences of union policy.

In this sense, we can say that the economy is apolitical or apolitical, despite the fact that it is the basis of politics and of any form of political activity. In addition, we can say that it is completely neutral for all valuations because it is always related to the methods and never to the choice of final objectives.

ECONOMIC RECOGNITION AND HUMAN ACTION

The freedom of human choice and action is limited three times. First, there are the laws of physics that your dishonest man must abide by in order to survive. Second, there are inherent constitutional characteristics and attitudes of the individual and the functioning of environmental factors; We know that this affects the choice of the end and the source, although our knowledge of how they work is rather vague. Finally, the regularity of phenomena related to the relationship between capacity and purpose, that is, the law of practice, is separate from the legislation of physics and physiology.

The enlightenment and the categorical and formal study of these third-class laws of the universe is the subject of practice and of the most developed industry to date. The body of economic knowledge is an essential element of the structure of human civilization; It is the foundation on which modern industry and all the moral, intellectual, technological and therapeutic achievements of recent centuries have been built. It depends on the men whether they use the rich treasure that this knowledge gives them, or whether they use it unused. But if they do not make the most of it and ignore its teachings and warnings, they are not destroying the economy; It will destroy society and humanity.

The context that life provides on a relative as well as the general level is the balance we all have in what we do and especially what we do not. After reading Walden Henry David Thoreau as a teenager, I could not read any further after stumbling across the line, "Most men live by silent desperation." Then I realized that his insights were in order. When I thought about it, I realized that the last thing I would ever do in such an emotional situation would be silence! This moment of revelation inspired me to become fully involved in this growing process of conscious living, and it made me interested in how universal this life is.

Human experience shows that we are much more equal than we are otherwise. Our diversity, which some describe as individual differences, is worth acknowledging. There is much that needs to be said to show respect and kindness to our diversity. At the same time, the ego-spirit always seems interested in differences of all kinds and is ready to doubt all the differences that are morally wrong and that separate a person from a group. another, a named group from another group. What if these 'differences' are exactly what is not 'the same'? Although this distinction seems purely linguistic and trivial, you need to look again and rethink the phrase that has the most emotional reactive charge and is relatively balanced in that regard. The answer is obvious. Everything common and universal to people, our similarities are much more an attraction and an influence on our lives. By noticing and appreciating our similarities and similarities, we challenge our poverty, our understanding, and our humanity.

The equations of life can be described as what everyone considers to be human beings. What are the major balance sheets in life? This is what everyone, without exception, experiences in the human experience of life on earth. This human equal provides the external environment and psychological context of our lives rather than the oceans that provide a life for the entire ocean. For example, the seriousness and limitations of physical reality, as well as living in the presence of the present and qualifying as a key balancer, affect us all. The awareness of equality brings a sharp relief to the playing field of human experience and the deep limitations on the development of our formation.

The best balance is probably to have contact with yourself and with each other. No matter how conscious and immediate you are, especially with your imaginary ego-spirit, to stand outside your mind and see what it has been up to now is available on a relatively global level. It certainly includes the fact of aging and death, as well as the ability to be present for yourself and yourself. While dealing with the events of aging and death, the books speak of how life is held and lived, while life represents death, as death represents life. It is strange to note that the number of times a person dies is a clear mirror.

At the same time, death can be seen as the ultimate abuse or irregularity, as only your body vehicle dies - it is not the shining core or what elevates your soul. Death can be viewed with the utmost accuracy as a step from self-freedom to our peaceful eternity with God, unity, and divinity. A key profile for all of us is the simple and temporary nature of the grand plan of earthly life and the timelessness of the conscious level.

It's so unique, if not a definite balance, to see life for what it is, and you can not do the opposite! To be clear, this view is not dependent on fate, fate, or karma. Rather, it is the realization that it is not the idea that our minds make use of the actual choice of how life works. Our proud association of the selfish mind with a true choice chooses four invincible consequences that completely disrupt the gut and chooses: (1) heredity, neuroscience, or genetic prediction; (2) ecological/social conditioning; (3) unconscious programs; and (4) how immediate or absent it is. By making conscious and adaptable, constructive lifestyle changes, comparing and resolving incompetent survival decisions based on environmental conditioning, becoming aware (suggested by Sigmund Freud as a cure for necrosis), and a greater presence itself, she is " rock "more in the" obvious choice ". Even in every moment of life and in actions that cannot be otherwise, there are many influences.

One of the great life plans is your health at every conceivable level. How do you take care of your body's physical health with diet, fitness, activity, rest, sleep, weight, and posture?

How do you maintain the emotional health of your heart and the cognitive health of your mind? When was the last time you stopped and thought deeply about your life path? What were you and how did you do it? Where do you come from here and now? Did you regret what you did not do, or regret it because you gave yourself the best 100% dedicated shot? What do you call living before the inevitable? And what do you want?

How do you maintain the health of your family members in close relationships with friends and family, in meaningful relationships with friends, and wonderful relationships with colleagues and acquaintances? Who thinks of anything different about their deathbeds than anyone else and everything they have ever dreamed of? Are you a good animal, a good land manager? How did you treat other living things and our earth? What living legacy do you leave behind?

How did you keep your physical environment, home, garden, and the surrounding community clean and tidy? What shape did your car drive? How often do you scrub under the bathroom cabinet or clean the tabletop and corners of the kitchen? When was the last time you ordered a desk, cupboard, garage, house, garden, yard, and office? When was the last time you went to work? Do not all these activities show your attitude towards yourself, others, the world, and life itself?

Your quality of happiness, success, prosperity, satisfaction, and contentment as a person is a good balance, as it is more related to what you create in feelings, thoughts, and attitudes than to something with circumstances, situations, and is. Another balance is how you are financially responsible in your professional and personal life. How can you communicate with the people around you, extended family members, co-workers, co-workers and service workers, friends, neighbors, and people you have never met?

Dealing with the inevitable loss of family members, material things, and money, as well as the limitations that arise at different stages of the aging process, is often a material balance. Have you left the world a little better to be here than if you've never been here before? Who made you permanent and significantly changed a person's quality of life? How many other outliers are known?

Your spirituality, as you mature your soul into the quality of your relationship and with God - where you end up in life and beyond - is the ultimate balance. Some refer to it by a universal phrase that has become more and more relevant over time: human experience. How are you currently aware of the equalizers of life? What do you add minute by minute to satisfy the big outliers?

JUDGING LIFE AND ITS VALUE

We can live - perhaps as animals - without judging whether it is good or bad, meaningless or meaningless, useful or not. But we do not. We judge the value of life and conclude that life has no value or value so that we can convince each other that we have a life right.

These judgments are not limited to philosophers. Many

people, whether they understand it or not, compare their life or life in general with their expectations or desires and then judge whether the life they have seen and seen corresponds to the standard they have. taken to test it. These ratings and ratings have a wide range of sophistication. On the one hand, there are simple statements, often quoted as 'life is good' or 'life is terrible', which may not be clear how the person came to the conclusion that they came. On the other hand, there are different judgments made by philosophers - these are often carefully examined, and based on complex arguments. Between these two extremes lie the evaluations and judgments of poets and playwrights, including well-known words that say that life is "full of noise and fury, which means nothing.

Various methods and standards have been removed and can be used to determine viability. In addition, our judgments about the value or the opposite of life are very much dependent on the method used, as shown. It is therefore important to pay attention to the examination of the methods used to assess this judgment.

Legal theorists have done a lot of work evaluating different courses of action, such as utilitarianism, and helping us decide between different actions. Conversely, little attention has been paid to the study of methods of determining the value of life. Instead, care is taken for years to determine whether a life without God and immortality can have meaning. In this article, I will explore different ways to evaluate and compare the value of life, with the ultimate goal of finding the best method for assessment.

PURPOSE IN TERMS OF VALUE AND WORTHINESS OF LIFE

When people first think of philosophical questions, they often start with purposeful questions such as "What does life mean?" and "Why are we here?" After considering these questions for a while, some people gradually find that these questions assume that life was created for a reason, and therefore they destroy the notion of understanding and ask a question. "Does life have a purpose?" As people ponder the famous question of the meaning of life, many people do not ask the simple question, "Is life worth living?" This is unfortunate for reasons I will explain.

Based on the literature on the question, "Does life have a purpose or a purpose? Is life worth living? One would think that the issue of purpose is more important. I do the opposite." Case is.

When I discuss the claim of some that life is not worth living if it has no meaning, I argue beyond any doubt that someone can find value even if their life is meaningless, regardless of whether it is considered important. as a universal meaning of 'hidden' or equally valuable or equally important. As for the second meaning, many lives are not valuable or important and have no meaning in this sense. But even that does not necessarily mean that it is not worth living. The opposite is also true. A person can lead a prosperous and functioning life, but a still life may not be worth living and may even commit suicide.

he plays with words and allows himself to believe that it is necessary to declare that it is not worth not giving meaning to life. In fact, there is no need for joint action between these two sets. Man, however, makes a common mistake by not distinguishing between these questions, the meaning of life, and the value of life.

For the questions "Is there a purpose in life?" and "Is life worth living?" The fact that one question can be answered negatively and the other positively, shows that these two questions differ. Some have pointed out that these are different concepts. The concept of what life is worth, for example, is separate from the concept that life has meaning.

While some philosophers have discovered that there is a difference between a "meaningful life" and a "life worth living," what distinguishes these concepts are not explored. What is the difference between these concepts? The main difference between these concepts is that the latter concept has a much wider scope than the previous one. A person who inquires about the meaning of life usually tries to know whether we were created for a purpose or whether we are playing a role in carrying out a divine or cosmic purpose or plan. It is a close matter of focused action. On the contrary, the question of whether life is worth living is broad. This question is often seen as a process of balancing benefit versus cost, good versus bad, or pleasure versus pain to determine whether the former is more important than the latter. The terminology of benefits and costs is used below.

Indeed, one of the benefits of life is the satisfaction that comes from achieving goals. However, life has other benefits, such as interacting with family and friends, appreciating music and art, and adventures that have nothing to do with focused or focused activity. Performance. If we ask ourselves, "Is life worth living?" These other benefits would be taken into account when considering life. But this will not happen if we only ask the question "Does life have a purpose?" and never asks the broadest and most important question: "Is life worth living?"

This includes judging whether life is worth living, not just whether someone has a "purpose" or a "purpose", regardless of how these words are interpreted, but also other experiences that are not a purpose is not. Since the appreciation of dignity is wider than the assessment of a goal, it explains how it is possible to lead a life that is not purposeful or purposeful, and yet is a life worth living. or to be. maybe. there to live a useful life and find out that life is not worth living.

"Life" as used in questions "Is there a purpose in life?" and "Is life worth living?" it can refer to life in general or our individual life. Therefore, it is necessary to define "life" when discussing these issues, to avoid misunderstandings. This essay contains the word "life" in the question "Is life worth living?" it relates to our individual life. This is an important question. The question is whether life, in general, is almost as strange and vague as the question, "Does life have a purpose?"

Of course, life in general does not last. It is individuals who survive, and therefore they are individuals, not life in general that is worth living. So the question is, "Is life (in general) worth living?". If asked, one might ask whether it is worth living the life of all who make up the human species. You also wonder if it is worth living the life of a normal or normal person, even if no one can have the character traits of this imaginary person.

The judgment that life is generally worthwhile has no practical value. If someone decides that his life is not worth living, that judgment can be applied by trying to engage in certain activities or relationships with others that add value to life. A person can also act on this judgment by ending his life. Life. However, if someone decides that life, in general, is not worth living, that person has little to do with judgment, except perhaps to make an open attempt to convince an entire population. the world to commit suicide.

The question "Does life have a purpose?" There are two possible answers: yes and no. None of these answers say anything about the value of our lives. However, one company faces the problem, arguing that life is of little value if life has no meaning, for example, says: "Without God, the universe is the result of a cosmic accident, an accidental explosion. There is no reason why it exists. For humans, it's a freak in nature: a blind product of material, more time, more possibilities. Man is but a piece of slime that has developed in his rationality. and others who make similar arguments suggest that there is a connection between the meaning of life and the value of our life. By claiming that life has no 'real' meaning or 'real' value if it has no purpose, they have adopted a purposeful standard to judge whether life has value.

What criteria or criteria should be used to assess whether our lives have any value? Should it be a purposeful standard or a performance standard? The two standards are as follows:

- My life is only valuable if human life has a purpose.
- My life is only valuable if the benefits of life outweigh the costs.

If we are to judge life, the standard by which we make judgments must be clear and cover a broad, if not all, experience. As stated before, the purposeful standard does not take into account non-objective experiences. Furthermore, the concept of "purpose", expressed in the statement that life has no value other than purpose, is not as vague as many people have claimed. Since there are different types of targets, this statement is confusing. It may have a purpose that somehow god or cosmos created human life for some reason (to fulfill a function). Alternatively, it may be a goal that was not created for us to serve the excellence of a function, but that we have chosen goals or a role ourselves, that we have chosen ourselves or implemented externally, with the goals to be achieved.) a supervisor.

Because the concept of a goal is vague and the assigned standard ignores many of our experiences - which we enjoy a lot - it is an inadequate measure to judge whether our lives are worth living. That being said, this standard is also based on the assumption that there is a direct connection between the divine or cosmic purpose and the value of our life, but is there such a relationship? If the cosmos was intelligent and has its purpose, such as continuous expansion, but man is unintentionally and merely a by-product of that expansion, then the fact that the cosmos has a purpose somehow contributes to our value of life. Some of them wonder if we would like to hear that we have a purpose, but that the purpose was to serve as a food source for another activity. The answer, of course, is 'no', which provides extra support that is not directly related to the question of whether human life was created for a reason and whether there is value in our lives.

One way to respond today to those who claim that life is without God and that immortality has no purpose is to point out that the word 'purpose' has two meanings and that a purpose can be created in your life by having a purpose. regardless of the fact. that life was created with a purpose. By pronouncing this alternative understanding of the word "purpose" and claiming that it is sufficient to understand life, these philosophers indirectly invoke a lower alternative standard to judge whether life has value. There does not have to be a great cosmic or divine purpose in which we play a central role in making a person's life precious. Instead, they suggest that having unnecessary, achievable goals and pursuing them with passion can add value to your life. Although the latter standard is clear and much more reasonable than the cosmic standard, like the cosmic standard, it is not short of experiences without deliberate action - experiences that would be included in a useful evaluation.

When the separate terms "value" and "length" are combined in the word "value", a powerful and elegant concept is created. Using this concept, the benefit and effort are taken into account by comparing them side by side to see if the benefit is justified by the effort. Since we have evolved into an imperfect natural world, where the creatures of the world compete for limited resources, which can lead to hunger, disease, and suffering, it is unrealistic to expect survival benefits alone. The performance standard recognizes that there is a cost of living and always will be, but not the objective standards. Therefore, the performance standard is a more realistic way to assess whether life has value above objective and performance standards.

METHODS FOR DETERMINING WHETHER LIFE IS WORTH LIVING

Method 1: Weighted Costs And Benefits

Although the performance standard has significant advantages over its efficiency in determining whether life is worth living, how can one determine whether life is worth living? It is possible to try to weigh the benefits of life, as mentioned earlier, against the cost. However, the cost-benefit analysis has revealed limitations, including the fact that it can be difficult to estimate benefits or costs. It can also be difficult to calculate benefits and costs. Therefore, it may not be possible to determine whether life offers a net benefit. Given the limitations of cost-benefit analyzes, it is important to explore alternative methods of assessing quality of life.

Others have used other distractions to find out if life is worth living. I will look at the different methods used or likely to be used to make this decision. Because you may be wondering if we can really understand the value of life, as suggested

We are always confronted with decisions about how we can best utilize the limited time as limited beings. We can imply, start and stop activities without considering whether the activities are useful, but generally not. We evaluate activities - before, during and after their implementation.

Let us first think about whether it is worthwhile before we start with the many activities we can do. And if we decide to start the business, we will not continue without thinking about it. Instead, we often ask ourselves if the activity is always worthwhile, and if it turns out not to be so, we will stop the activity unless we are forced to continue or be afraid of what might happen if we do it. will do. stop. Before we start trading again, we need to consider whether the original activity is worthwhile. If we realized that the original activity was a 'waste of time', it would not repeat itself. If we find the original activity useful, it can be repeated.

Normally we do not make decisions about starting, continuing or repeating an action impulsively or without thinking rationally. Instead, we evaluate whether the activity is worth starting, continuing, or repeating. If we're starting or running a business, you'll probably understand that it was worth it. And if we repeat an action, it means that the original action is useful to us. But how can we determine if we are worthy of our individual life as a whole? Can we discuss the methods above to find out if an activity is worthwhile and to determine if we are worth living? As indicated, this is the approach of some.

We have not made a decision to be born into this world (a point that many existentialists emphasize), nor can we repeat our lives. Based on these choices, we can therefore not know whether it is worth living for us. However, we can imagine that we would make the decision to start a life and live our lives if we made the choice. In addition, it is conceivable for a person to repeat a person's life if possible. After all, can you imagine that we can find out if it's worth living based on whether we should keep living or not? These methods are discussed below to determine the best way to determine viability.

In a previous article, we evaluated the methods based on the purpose and method of earnings, as well as the standards derived from these methods. They were judged for clarity and took into account several of our experiences. All five methods of inference discussed (methods two to six) are all fairly clear and comprehensive. Two additional criteria are considered in the assessment, including: (1) whether the method can validly determine the validity of a person's life and (2) whether the standard is suitable for the application of the method. The best way to judge the value of life is revealed in the last section.

Method 2: Stay Alive

The fact that pessimists continue to live their lives and participate in projects, as Scripture suggests, can be argued that, despite the opposite assertion, they are finding a life worth living. But does the fact that you are not finished with your life show that you are worth living? People do not die fast, as evidenced by the drastic measures people take to commit suicide, such as jumping out of tall buildings. People can continue to live on a miserable level instead of ending their lives in fear of death. It is often said that a man will end his life if the fear of life overcomes the fear of death. Death, however, fears much resistance: you stand like a guard at the exit gate. In other words, people can not live because they think it is worth living, but for other reasons: because they fear death and the pain that would result from suicide, or because they have hope. with. that at some point in life they may become worth living. If this is true, we can not rightly conclude that it is worth living just because we go on with our lives.

People are cursed with a conscious awareness of their death.

Humans, unlike other species, are cursed with a conscious awareness of their mortality. I believe that the tragedy of the human condition is that people's awareness and true awareness of this external problem contributes to the final irony: humanity is brilliant and offensive, sensitive and brutal, genuinely caring and painfully uninteresting, extremely creative, and exaggerated about themselves and to destroy others. The ability to imagine and conceptualize you has both negative and positive consequences because it conveys states of anxiety that end up in a defensive form of denial.

The tragedy is that the protection that enables us to survive the emotional pain of childhood and outward despair is not only inadequate and limits our potential to lead a full life, but it inevitably leads to negative behavior toward others. and thus creates a destructive cycle... Paradoxically, religious ideologies and beliefs that are a source of spiritual comfort, relief from a sense of unity, and interpersonal suffering, polarize toward one another. Threatened by people of different customs and religious systems, we mistakenly believe that we should overwhelm or destroy them.

With all the advances in science and technology, if one portrays the state of the world correctly today, it must be regarded as complete madness. Millions of people are hungry, genocide reaches epic proportions, ethnic conflicts and prejudices are omnipotent, there are mass murders in the name of religion, and war remains a viable solution to our differences. With better, more efficient, less causal weapons and the superior rationality of technology, human life on the planet can be destroyed.

Emotion and empathy are an important part of our human heritage, but when we experience great and urgent pain, we develop precautions to keep our suffering to a minimum. We are separated from our emotions and are desensitize and are more likely to become destructive or attack others. Changing this negative legacy requires deep psychological knowledge and empathy, as well as faith and determination to pursue this endeavor against all contradictions.

With a deep understanding and the feeling that we all have the same destiny and the knowledge that death is the greatest level, there is hope that there will be a worldview characterized by respect, love, and care for all our members. We believe that we can have a positive impact on the fate of mankind in a positive direction by learning how people are later harmed and protected, by gradually eliminating incomplete parenting practices and gaining a better understanding. let's go to human nature and fringe.

In this regard, understanding the philosophical issues of an ethical approach to life requires a thorough understanding of human psychology and especially the importance of protective education. The repellents introduced during childhood as a necessity to live psychologically also prevent the formation and survival of true moral life. Personal harm caused by excessive criticism, rejection, or by hostility from parents, predicts that children will become adults who hurt others. There is no way to defend an innocent person if someone has not lived alone. Whether we know it or not, the ways we trust and distort others do significant damage. It hurts the people closest to us, especially our children, and then it stretches.

After all, society is a set of individual psychological defenses, and it is the defenses and the consequent damage they have done to others that are inflicted across the world. It manifests in the failure to empathize and empathize with others, total prejudice, ethnic cleansing, and religious warfare. Proper education about our psychological defenses, how they form, and how they work, is essential to gain an understanding of the content of ethics. It is unlikely that a person who lives harmoniously within himself will protect and respect others; he raises a hand to hurt others. People with an open mind can create a peaceful world that reflects care and equality for all.

Despite our differences, we live on the same finite planet. We depend on solar energy, clean air, and clean water, plants, and animals of the world. We work the land and follow many of the same principles as horticulture and agriculture. We marvel at the stars and the sky itself and the beauty and power of nature touches us. We are affected by the same forces of nature like wind, rain, and storm. Our lives are centered daily and influenced by the world's weather conditions and seasons.

Despite our differences, we age and are aware of aging and death. We experience aging in the same way: skin folds shrink, our muscles shrink and soften, our body slows down, our organs deteriorate. As we get older, we gain special wisdom and embrace that we always have more.

Despite our differences, we still live our lives surrounded by others. We accept some of them and have a special love for others we call 'friends'. We depend on our friends, and they, us, for their comfort and company. We ask for advice and give advice. We compensate them and forget about their shortcomings because we know they are doing it for us. We feel loyal to them.

Despite our differences, we are surrounded by the products and effects of humanity. Every street and every path, every window, every belt, and every shoe, every building, every fence, every nail, and every garden; Aircraft and cars on the way; Every porch, every phone, every chair, every book, every shirt, every cigarette, every tin, every screwdriver, every traffic sign, every computer, every ship, every piece of paper or every flagpole - this is the product and the effect of mankind. The noises on the streetcars and buses, men and women talking, hammers, heavy equipment screaming for food, children crying, music from homes and shops - these are the products and effects of humanity. Even our ideas "play out" in a language that is not ours, but a product of humanity.

The human experience is largely a shared experience. When you hear the sound of traffic in front of a window, or the sounds of children playing, or the television or radio playing in the background, or the roar of the frames, do not think so. same for the man who read it in Canada or Frankfort? - or for the woman reading it in Toronto?

Despite our differences, we have love and sexual desire; We find friends, create, and father children. We respond to the same comforting or funny look - laughter - or those weird, involuntary bursts in the lungs, laughter. We embrace times of relaxation, relaxation, comfort, and well-being because we know that life is uncertain - that fatigue, frustration, willpower, depression, sadness, or desire are no less.

All these aspects of human life, despite their many differences, are the same for all mankind. There are also differences here - important; But just as there are differences, there are other and innumerable examples of our common humanity. The one is not exclusive to the other; both are "at work"; We influence each other every day for the rest of our lives.

Every book and word is proof of the general knowledge and experiences of mankind. Any glasses; any pill; Bottled beer or soft drinks; any bicycles or cars; every song, poem, weapon. From the use of spoons to the use of computers, from floating knowledge to knowledge of the principles of quantum mechanics. . .

The bridge is a product that you cross to get to work or that you can travel with to visit a friend or family member what? From the general knowledge of mankind to reliable technology, building practices and materials, precise measurements, and mathematical formulations to the legislation of physics. Does this not also apply to the bridges of North Korea, Australia, Nigeria, and Belgium? And can the same not be said for dams, tunnels, bridges, and other structures in Peru, the USA.

Mankind's general knowledge of engineering, mathematics, engineering, and construction practices and the laws of physics is influenced, protected, influenced, and known for the lives of all people. However, these are just four relatively small areas in the vast world of human knowledge: a common area of knowledge that exists will continue to grow despite our differences.

It's easy to see, isn't it? Much of what ordinary people do, give, know or experience despite their differences is an important part of everyone's 'separate' life - which is very important for their happiness, their success and success, their happiness and the success of their loved ones?

Without clearing up my differences - me, me, or anyone else - ask yourself: where would I place my ability and my desire for friendship or my love of nature or my ability to obtain and interact with information? to have, instead? communicate through? of words and symbols or my feelings for my child - or where I was born into a world where I or my family members can be saved through life-saving drugs or medical procedures developed by mankind - or that we can be saved (My family and I live in a world where others have developed and shared a wealth of products and knowledge that make life easier, safer and more productive or even because of the pain and disappointment in my life and empathy with others who have been hurt), became ill or discouraged - where would I mention these and other general aspects of the person, if I tried to name all the aspects of my experience - that is, those that are shared and those that are not shared, What role do these common things play in my overall ability (or later, my child) to enjoy life, function successfully in society, and love and support others? These examples may not be on top of the list not (not important knot). But any solemn person surely adds these and other general aspects of human experience to their list. These are certainly important human qualities.

The companion flag is a simple proof of identity. This means that what is the same in all of us and all of us, is an integral part of the comparison in all of human life. This is not the only part; it does not transcend our differences and may not be as important as some of our differences, but it still fits these differences in a ubiquitous home. The acceptance of the Community flag means that the people of the world agree: it is worth symbolizing this fact alone - the fact of our common humanity: it is worth having a tangible and eternal memory before our eyes and in the sight of us to have children, and to face the eyes of all generations. come, do not forget, reject or forget - our common bond.

THE LIFE OF A HUMAN AND THE PROBLEM WE FACE EVERYDAY

As humans, we have made significant progress that we could not even imagine almost a century ago. The wonders of modern technology have given us tremendous power over the forces of nature. We have been through many disasters, but the last question is, "Are we happier than our ancestors were in the past?" The answer is no '.

The abuse of women, children, and religious and racial discrimination continues to be harmed; the color bars and caste discrimination do not decrease. People who enjoy relevant refreshments may suffer more than their 'poor' peers. Mental illness, stress, and loneliness are some of the serious problems we are currently experiencing in modern society. But the crucial question is: who is responsible for all the evils that plague the world today? " '

Many people want to take credit for the progress that mankind has made. Religions, scientists, politicians, and economists immediately claim that mankind owes them a fortune. But who is to blame? I think everyone is equally responsible. Let us turn our attention and ask ourselves to say honestly whether we were also responsible for not bringing peace and happiness to our fellow man.

We are all responsible for some of the horrors that take place in the middle of the day because we are too scared, to tell the truth. For example, we try to cultivate man's desire for sensory satisfaction. Thanks to the grace of money and power, unscrupulous people have developed a multimillion-dollar industry to provide sensory pleasure in every way and to capture and sacrifice young children.

Mankind has never before been free from conflict, bad feelings, self-control, decency, and conflict. We urgently need peace, not only in our personal lives at home and at work, but also in the world. Not only does it overwhelm the tension, anxiety, and fear associated with conflict, it threatens our well-being, mentally as well as physically. To have a huge impact on everything around them, people are now among the most violent people in the world. To some extent, they succeeded but paid a terrible price for it. They sacrifice peace of mind for material comfort and strength.

The fundamental problem we face today is moral decay and misuse of information. Despite all the advances in science and technology, the world is much safer and more peaceful. Science and technology have made human life more uncertain than ever. If there are no spiritual improvements in the way we deal with our problems, there is a danger that humanity itself will be destroyed.

The world religions have always claimed that human happiness depends only on the satisfaction of physical desires and passions or on the acquisition of material wealth and power. Although we all have worldly joys, we can still not be happy and peaceful if our minds are always concerned about the fear and hatred that results from ignorance about the true nature of life.

True happiness cannot be defined in terms of wealth, power, children, smoking, or inventions. Undoubtedly, it provides temporary physical and spiritual comfort, but may not ultimately provide lasting happiness. This is especially true if the property is acquired illegally or through abuse. It is a source of pain, guilt, and sadness instead of giving the owner happiness.

We are too often led to believe that the joy of the five senses can ensure happiness. Beautiful places, magical music, fragrant scents, wonderful tastes, and a seductive body touches deceive and deceive us just to enslave us of worldly pleasures. Although no one will deny that immediate happiness is the expectation of joy and the satisfaction of the senses, such joys are awaited. If one sees these joys objectively, then you understand the incessant and unsatisfactory nature of these joys. It gives you a better understanding of personal responsibility: what this life means and how to achieve true happiness!

We can only develop and maintain inner peace by turning our minds inward rather than outward. We need to be aware of the dangers and pitfalls of the destructive forces of greed, hatred, and rhythm. We must learn to cultivate and maintain good forces of kindness, love, and harmony. The core of the battle lies in us and we are not fighting with weapons or other resources, but with our spiritual awareness of all the negative and positive forces present in our head.

Consciousness makes a man drunk. A drunk man speaks openly. And like a parachute, the mind works best when fully open. This awareness is the key to opening the door to conflict and confrontation, as well as valid ideas that arise.

The spirit is the ultimate source of all happiness and misery. To have happiness in the world, the human mind must first be calm and happy. Individual happiness contributes to the happiness of society, and the happiness of society means the happiness of the nation. The happiness of this world is based on the happiness of nations. Here we need a network photo. Think of the whole universe as one big network with one node on each network. If we break a knot, the whole network will be shaken. Everyone should make the world happy.

The lessons from life show that real victory can only be achieved through confrontation. Success is never achieved through conflict. Happiness never comes from bad feelings. Peace is never achieved by accumulating wealth or gaining world power. Peace is only brought about by abandoning our identity and helping the world with acts of love. Peace of mind is about all opposition. It also helps us to maintain healthy minds and lead rich and fulfilling lives with happiness and contentment. "As wars are fought in the minds of the people, the stronghold of peace must be built in the minds of the people.

Especially in many so-called prosperous societies, people today have more problems, dissatisfaction, and intellectual disabilities than in underdeveloped societies. This is because men are addicted to their sensory pleasure and seek worldly pleasure without adequate moral and spiritual development. Their tension, fear, anxiety, and insecurity disturb their minds. This situation is the biggest problem in many countries. Since people in developed societies have not learned to maintain contentment in their lives, they will naturally be unhappy.

There are four areas in which a man tries to achieve his life goal:

- Material or physical level;

-Satisfied and uncomfortable or pleasant or uncomfortable;

- Study and motivation;

-A comprehensive understanding based on pure justice and fair treatment,

The latter is the realistic and permanent method that never leads to disappointment. People today need more wealth not only to fulfill their lives and obligations but also because their accumulated disgust has increased. Now it's a kind of competition.

To have worldly pleasure, there must be an external object or feast, but to find spiritual happiness, it is not necessary to have such an external object.

Many young people have lost confidence and find it difficult to do so in their lives. The main cause of this spiritual attitude is excessive ambition and fear, which leads to competition, jealousy, and uncertainty. Such problems naturally create a very bad atmosphere for others who want to live peacefully. The fact is that when someone creates a problem, his behavior affects the well-being of others.

An animal is never happy but enjoys it. Happiness is not based on your random gratification, but on sacrificing joy for others.

To most people, a person is a rich person, community, or nation that is 'rich' in the sense of goods or money that represents material profit. Originally, the word "prosperity" meant a state of well-being. The word "Commonwealth" has this meaning. But it is now used to refer to a quality that promotes substantial well-being in general, rather than a state of mind of well-being.

Of course, we can not deny that the desire for wealth is a valuable adjustment to success if kept within reasonable limits. Desire itself is not bad. Unbridled desire, however, leads to unbridled desire, jealousy, greed, fear, and cruelty toward others. Raising money can help bring about a kind of happiness, but it does not satisfy alone. When most men fail with great potential if they waste the source to the end. They do not understand the nature, meaning, and proper functioning of wealth, which is merely a 'resource' to end the highest happiness. But you can be happy without being rich. An old Chinese story will illustrate this.

There was once a king who wanted to learn how to be truly happy. One of his pastors told him that he should wear a shirt from a man who was very happy to be happy. After a long time, he found such a man, but the lucky one has no shirt to give to the king. That's why he was happy!

Wealth must be used wisely and wisely. It must be used for the benefit of one person as well as for the benefit of another. If someone spends his time clinging to his property without fulfilling his obligations to his country, people, and religions, he will experience an awful empty plague. Too many people are content with material gain until they forget their responsibility to their families and fellow human beings. Happiness is a strange thing. The more you share it, the more satisfaction you will get.

If someone is selfish and it's time to leave the world, they will realize that they have not reached their full wealth. No one, not even a rich person, will benefit greatly from the accumulated wealth.

Some people think that they can overcome their problems by gaining more and more wealth. So they try to be billionaires, they work hard, but after becoming billionaires, they face many other unexpected problems: insecurity, unrest, enemies, and the difficulty of maintaining their wealth. It clearly shows that building wealth is not the solution to human problems. Undoubtedly, wealth can help overcome certain problems, but all the joy in the world cannot be achieved with money. Money cannot eliminate natural problems.

Philosophers, great thinkers, and rationalists have formulated the nature of human weaknesses and how to overcome them. However, many people see them only as theories and not as solutions to their problems. Sometimes the intellect creates more problems because it increases our selfish perception of ourselves.

The man at the center of the universe was long ago seen as

the most important inhabitant. According to this view, the world was created for humans so that they could get what they wanted out of it because it was the creatures they liked best, and it was a great pleasure for them to have everything on this planet.

The so-called 'humanitarian' attitude is possibly directly responsible for the heinous rape of our planet and disregard for the rights of others with us. For example, there have been tragic situations in which some animal species are exterminated due to the unnecessary killing of unsympathetic people to pursue their sporting pursuits or business goals. Even today, science and technology claim to place nature beneath nature. We need the number of people among us who have already contributed to the tremendous destruction destroyed by humans in the name of 'progress'. Nature has hitherto been very good at confirming this and has enabled man to continue to think that this planet has been raped and plundered by the will to satisfy its irrevocable greed for material goods and satisfaction. There are many warning signs today that the pleasant times are coming to an end. I hope that if compassion and true vision do not save the world, the same uniqueness and desire for self-preservation and complacency will force us to think wisely about our poor environment and our other suffering beings on this earth.

Man is biologically weaker than anyone, big or small. Other animals are born armed with some sort of weapon to protect and survive. On the contrary, people put everything in the foreground, but not as a weapon. Humans are considered living beings because they are meant to harmonize with others but not to destroy them. They found religion for this purpose. Everything that makes people alive and alive has the same vitality. They are part of the same cosmic energy that takes different forms during infinite rebirths, from human to animal, to divine form and back, inspired by the powerful existential slip (survival instinct) that guides them from birth to death and rebirth. again in an infinite cycle called samsara. The three sources of male injuries that bind him to samsara are greed, hatred, and disappointment.

THE AIM OF THE STUDY

It is a great tragedy in human life that many people go through life without being able to express their potential meaningfully. on the other hand, notes that some are so focused on making money that they tend to forget to live.

The above insight inspired this research. The seeker therefore wants to wake up to those who have not yet introduced or enjoyed the latest opportunities, and are those who have lost hope of realizing meaning in life as furious about their excessive obsession or addiction to work so hard to to remind them that Kierkegaard was right when he said 'until man understands his essential self in God, that his life is full of worries, he is confident that all this knowledge or wisdom will have difficulty in being one thing live to make everything better and not bitter, this work aims to make everyone aware that human life is meaningful, as it is subjectively pursued through the person's personal experiences, correct understanding and use of freedom, solemn fear and for the Creator.

JUSTIFICATION OF THE STUDY OF THE STUDY

The daily human challenges at all levels have profound consequences, and more and more complications are becoming available to us to pursue sustainable lifestyle trends. Because of the weaknesses in human verification in almost every aspect of a person's life or society, he or she or the other person is almost a blind copy. The everyday problems in life usually separate us from self-realization to fully understand ourselves and tackle the problems that affect our nature to achieve our goals in a changing and changing world. . A man often focuses on reflecting on others at the expense of his unique individuality. Instead of being an authentic person who questions the freedom, meaning and handling of the existential phenomenon of death, suffering, horror, despair, absurdity, etc. Answer, the person melts in the crowd in a different way and in that way it loses its individuality to the person. an abstract goal to achieve or control the business. Kierkegaard's opposition to this tendency and his answer to the question "What does it mean to be human?" In this research, an energetic question raises their understanding of human life. In this way, the logic behind this research is preserved and its influence in modern man on reality, as it already exists, is remembered.

It helps man to achieve his purpose of existence by shaping his life by realizing and reflecting on himself by excluding himself from the crowd.

this proposal of three phases of life will help a modern person to realize that it is the understanding that life means that he is an individual who tries, thinks about alternatives, chooses, decides and acts, with more importance to ensure existential commitment . , worth making a healthy, critical, daring, daring and analytical person while making decisions throughout his life.

It is also relevant for modern man to focus the modern world on the fact that self-realization and evaluation can only be made when a man makes a personal decision based on deep personal reflection and the free exercise of his willpower and is willing to take responsibility for his subjective decisions about the objective audience that follows.

Also consider the scope of epistemology that deals with the nature, scope and criteria of knowledge. The research contributes a lot to the epistemology by revealing this knowledge that qualifies for such a conclusion about human nature. It also awakens the sleeping man who takes responsibility and creates its origin or meaning, even if he experiences problems, that may have happen in the past or in the present times of existence.

The human problem is known in the context of this freedom. Their respective uses and abuses confuse a man. This access is about freedom and the central point is what a man affirms. His report on this is the classification as an authentic or non-technological person. It is most commendable to measure the meaning or meaning of life, but in either case it is determined by the degree of commitment one has to assert himself before exercising freedom.

www.ingramcontent.com/pod-product-compliance
Lightning Source LLC
Chambersburg PA
CBHW060108260726
48658CB00004B/1466